THE CLASSIC AMERICAN
QUILT COLLECTION™
◊
NINE PATCH

Series Editor
Mary V. Green

 Rodale Press, Emmaus, Pennsylvania

Our Mission

We publish books that empower people's lives.

RODALE BOOKS

Executive Editor: *Margaret Lydic Balitas*
Managing Editor and Series Development: *Suzanne Nelson*
Senior Associate Editor: *Mary V. Green*
Technical Writer: *Janet Wickell*
Quilt Scout: *Bettina Havig*
Copy Editor: *Carolyn Mandarano*

Copy Manager: *Dolores Plikaitis*
Office Manager: *Karen Earl-Braymer*
Administrative Assistant: *Susan Nickol*
Art Director: *Michael Mandarano*
Cover and Interior Designer: *Denise M. Shade*
Book Layout: *Carol Angstadt and Lisa Palmer*
Photographer: *Mitch Mandel*
Illustrators: *Mario Ferro, Charles Metz, and Jackie Walsh*

If you have any questions or comments concerning this book, please write to:
   Rodale Press, Inc.
   Book Readers' Service
   33 East Minor Street
   Emmaus, PA 18098

Library of Congress Cataloging-in-Publication Data

The Classic American quilt collection. Nine patch / Mary V. Green, series editor.
   p. cm.
   ISBN 0–87596–643–8 hardcover
   1. Patchwork—United States—Patterns.
2. Quilting—United States—Patterns. 3. Patchwork quilts—United States. I. Green, Mary V.
TT835.C59   1994
746.46—dc20   94–19175
                                                      CIP

Distributed in the book trade
by St. Martin's Press
2 4 6 8 10 9 7 5 3   hardcover

CONTENTS

Acknowledgments

Oklahoma Nine Patch, made by Carolyn Miller, Santa Cruz, California. Carolyn was inspired to create this quilt when she saw a similar one in a small photo in a book on Oklahoma heritage quilts. Except for adding the border, she pieced and quilted it entirely by hand. Carolyn was a quiltmaker for years before deciding in 1987 to, as she puts it, "make quilts seriously." She has since won several ribbons at local shows. Her favorite projects are heavily quilted scrap quilts.

Double Nine Patch, made by Sharyn Craig, El Cajon, California. Sharyn is a nationally known quiltmaker, teacher, and author who enjoys challenging other quiltmakers to exercise their creativity. She made this quilt as a class sample of a Double Nine-Patch block set with sashing strips rather than with alternating squares. This quilt is now owned by Sharyn's mother, Pauline Squier.

Four Patch/Nine Patch, made by Marie Fritz, San Diego, California. Marie made this quilt and two others like it after admiring a similar quilt made by her friend, quiltmaker and author Blanche Young. Marie was a potter before she discovered quilting in 1979 and got hooked for life. To date she has made more than 50 quilts and there is "no end in sight." This quilt was machine quilted by Shirley Greenhoe and is owned by Marie's daughter, Diana Fickas.

Snowball and Nine Patch, made by Carolyn Miller, Santa Cruz, California. Since Carolyn was making this quilt for her son, Matthew, she chose "masculine" colors and a simple pattern that left lots of room for elaborate quilting. Carolyn prefers to hand piece and hand quilt her projects, as she finds the process relaxing.

Mennonite Four Patch/Nine Patch, owned by Joan Townsend, Lebanon, Ohio. Joan has been buying and selling antique quilts for more than 15 years. She is the proprietor of Oh Suzanna, a Lebanon, Ohio, shop specializing in antiques and linens.

Dots and Dashes, made by Sharyn Craig, El Cajon, California. Sharyn was inspired to create this quilt after she saw a photo of an antique pillow in a magazine and decided that its design would look great as a quilt. She is proud of the fact that the whole quilt top is made of leftovers recycled from two earlier quilt projects.

Wild Geese, owned by Shirley McElderry, Ottumwa, Iowa. Shirley discovered this quilt top in an antique shop near Muscatine, Iowa, and quilted it herself. She's been a quiltmaker since the 1950s and is an avid collector of antique quilts and fabrics. For the past 15 years, Shirley has used some of her extensive collection of fabrics to repair antique quilts for collectors and dealers all over the country.

Summer's End, made by Judy Miller, Columbia, Maryland. This quilt is the happy result of an idea that, according to Judy, had been "simmering in me for quite awhile." Combining scraps she had on hand with fabrics purchased at summer sales, she created a contemporary-looking quilt using a traditional pattern and setting. The quilt was exhibited at the Quilter's Heritage Celebration in Lancaster, Pennsylvania, in 1993, where it was awarded an Honorable Mention. Judy has been quilting since 1977, when she made a quilt from embroidered blocks she had started 20 years earlier.

Antique Double Nine Patch, owned by Cindy Rennels, Clinton, Oklahoma. No history is available about this lovely 1930s-era quilt. It appears here courtesy of Cindy, the proprietor of Cindy's Quilts in Clinton, Oklahoma. Cindy has been collecting and dealing with antique quilts for the past eight years.

On the Road Again . . . Paducah Bound, made by Nancy Chizek, Ann Arbor, Michigan. Nancy created this quilt for a challenge project in which the black and dark gray fabrics were provided. This was her first attempt at free-motion machine quilting. She's been quilting for about 14 years and says she enjoys all aspects of the process, "especially buying the fabric." Nancy uses both hand and machine techniques for piecing, appliqué, and quilting.

Magic Cross Nine Patch, owned by Cindy Rennels, Clinton, Oklahoma. Cindy obtained this quilt from an estate in Sarcoxie, Missouri. She is an avid collector and enjoys searching for quilts in a variety of colors, patterns, and techniques. Cindy especially enjoys meeting other people who appreciate quilts as much as she does.

Perkiomen Valley Split Nine Patch, owned by Nancy Roan, Bechtelsville, Pennsylvania. Nancy has been around quilts and quilting her entire life and has been making quilts herself since the late 1960s. With her husband, Donald ("Abe"), she authored *Lest I Shall Be Forgotten,* a book chronicling the quilting heritage of the Pennsylvania Dutch. She is an active member of the Variable Star Quilters, a group whose accomplishments include publishing *The Quiltie Ladies' Scrapbook* and the *W.P.A. Museum Project of Quilt Patterns.*

INTRODUCTION

For countless years, tiny fingers clutching needle and thread have learned the basics of piecing by stitching small squares together into simple Nine-Patch blocks. While mothers and grandmothers patiently supervised, important lessons were learned about color and design as well as accurate cutting and careful sewing. The completed blocks could then be joined together to make a doll quilt—a treasure to be played with and loved for many years to come. In this way, the humble Nine Patch often kindled the flame of a lifelong passion for quiltmaking.

The Nine-Patch design made its earliest appearances in the second quarter of the nineteenth century. Great technological advances during this period, particularly the introduction of roller-printed fabric, had a huge impact on the textile industry. The new process made available a larger variety of fabrics in greater quantity than ever before. Quiltmakers seized this exciting opportunity, and new patterns, such as the Nine Patch, Four Patch, and a number of star patterns, began to emerge almost immediately. Most of these new designs contained many small pieces, providing a perfect opportunity to take advantage of the many new fabrics available.

Through the years, the Nine Patch has endured as one of America's favorite and most versatile quilt patterns. Even today, the basic three-by-three grid of plain, equal-size squares is often one of the first patterns taught to beginning quilters, and it's easy to see why. It is an uncomplicated pattern with tremendous potential for variation. Whether set straight or on point, with alternate blocks or with sashing strips, there are almost limitless design possibilities. Through creative use of color, setting, and size, the result can range from a sweet and simple doll quilt to the strong graphic image of a boldly colored Amish bed quilt.

Over the years, a vast number of new and different quilt designs—variations on the basic block—have evolved, a testament to the unending creativity of quiltmakers. The possibilities multiply even further when the nine sections of the block are divided up into different-size segments or combined with elements such as appliqué.

In the pages of this book, you'll find a varied and appealing collection of quilts, all with one thing in common: Whether made up of plain squares or pieced segments, all of the quilts presented fall into the same general category—that of nine equal squares arranged in three rows of three. From the pure simplicity of the Double Nine Patch on page 10 to the challenge posed by the tiny pieces of the Magic Cross Nine Patch on page 86, there's a quilt here sure to inspire every quilter. And while most Nine-Patch quilts are relatively easy to construct, there are different levels of complexity. With that thought in mind, we've assigned each project a skill level in relation to the other projects in this book. For example, while the Magic Cross quilt may not be challenging in relation to a classic Mariner's Compass or a Feathered Star, it is more difficult than the Wild Geese project on page 52.

So page through the projects and choose one to start right now. Maybe there's a young girl in your life who's ready to share your interest in quilting—here's a great way to get her started. Maybe you want a design challenge to stretch your creative muscles—these patterns are perfect. Whatever your reason, there's no better time than now to add this true American classic to your own quilt collection. Happy quilting!

Mary Green

Mary Green

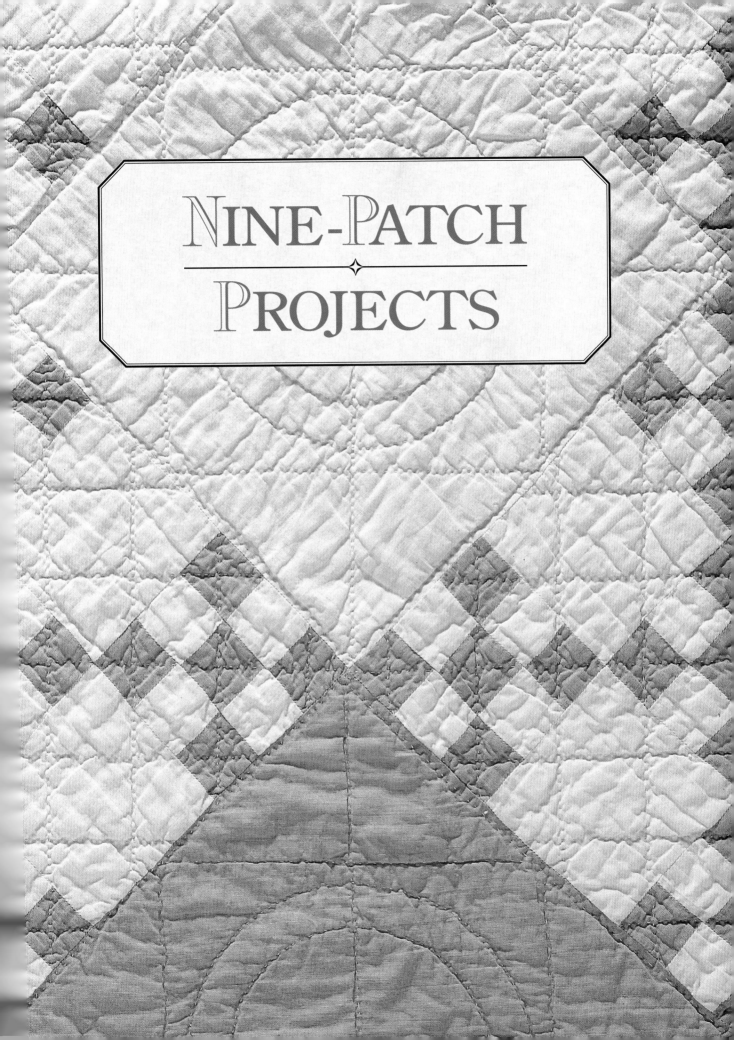

NINE-PATCH
PROJECTS

OKLAHOMA NINE PATCH

Skill Level: *Easy*

This dynamic scrap quilt was inspired by a photo in a book on Oklahoma heritage quilts. Since the pattern could not be identified, the quiltmaker named it in honor of its source. In this double-size version, the interaction of black and white creates a striking three-dimensional effect and forms a perfect backdrop for the explosion of color resulting from the dozens of scrap fabrics used.

Before You Begin

Each Double Nine-Patch block in this quilt is composed of five Nine-Patch blocks and four triangle squares. The directions are written based on using an easy strip-piecing technique for making the Nine-Patch blocks. Strips of fabric are sewn together into strip sets. The strip sets are then cut apart and resewn into blocks. Read through the general construction directions in "Nine-Patch Basics," beginning on page 102, for further details on strip piecing.

The directions for making the triangle squares are based on using the grid method. You will cut 10½-inch strips into squares, layer two squares together, and then mark and cut the grid as directed.

Choosing Fabrics

If you want to re-create the look of the quilt shown, use as many different fabrics as possible for the Nine-Patch blocks. The directions are written so that each pair of dark and light strips will result in three Nine-Patch blocks.

Quilt Sizes

	Lap	Double (shown)
Finished Quilt Size	57" × 79½"	79½" × 102"
Finished Block Size		
Double Nine Patch	11¼"	11¼"
Small Nine Patch	3¾"	3¾"
Triangle Squares	3¾"	3¾"
Number of Blocks		
Double Nine Patch	24	48
Small Nine Patch	120	240
Triangle Squares	96	192

Materials

	Lap	Double
Assorted darks	2⅛ yards	4 yards
Assorted lights	2⅛ yards	4 yards
Black	1⅝ yards	2⅝ yards
White	1⅛ yards	2 yards
Dark print	1⅛ yards	1½ yards
Backing	5 yards	7½ yards
Batting	63" × 86"	86" × 108"
Binding	⅝ yard	¾ yard

NOTE: Yardages are based on 44/45-inch-wide fabrics that are at least 42 inches wide after preshrinking.

For best results, use two new fabrics for each pair. If you do use a fabric more than once, be sure to pair it up with a different fabric each time.

To help develop your own

Cutting Chart

Fabric	Used For	Strip Width	Number of Strips Lap	Number of Strips Double
Assorted darks	Strip sets	1¾"	40	80
Assorted lights	Strip sets	1¾"	40	80
Black	Triangle squares	10½"	3	6
	Inner border	2½"	7	9
White	Triangle squares	10½"	3	6
Dark print	Outer border	4½"	7	9

unique color scheme for the quilt, photocopy the **Color Plan** on page 9, and use crayons or colored pencils to experiment with different color arrangements.

Light and dark yardages shown are generous estimates of the total yardage used in the quilt. Since small amounts of many fabrics are a key ingredient for a successful scrap quilt, you will likely begin with more yardage than indicated, but not all of it will be used.

CUTTING

All measurements include ¼-inch seam allowances. Referring to the Cutting Chart, cut the required number of strips in the width needed. Cut all strips across the fabric width (crosswise grain).

Cut the black and white fabrics for the triangle squares into 10½-inch-wide strips, then cut the strips into 10½-inch squares. Pair up one white and one black square for each grid of triangle squares.

Note: Cut and piece one sample block before cutting all the fabric for the quilt.

PIECING THE BLOCKS

Each Double Nine-Patch block is made up of five Nine-Patch blocks and four triangle squares, as illustrated in the **Block Diagram.** The scrappy Nine-Patch blocks are assembled using easy strip-piecing techniques. The triangle squares are made using the grid method.

Block Diagram

Making the Triangle Squares

Step 1. Working on the wrong side of a 10½-inch white square, use a pencil or permanent marker to draw a grid of four 4⅝-inch squares, as shown in **Diagram 1A.** Draw the grid so that it is at least ½ inch from the raw edges of the fabric. Referring to **1B**, carefully draw a diagonal line through each square in the grid.

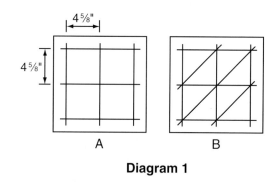

Diagram 1

Step 2. Place the white square right sides together with a 10½-inch black square. Using a ¼-inch seam allowance, stitch along both sides of the diagonal lines, as shown in **Diagram 2**. Use the edge of your presser foot as a ¼-inch guide, or draw a line ¼ inch from each side of the diagonal line.

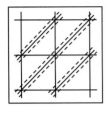

Diagram 2

Step 3. Use a rotary cutter and ruler to cut the grid apart. See page 115 in "Quiltmaking Basics" for complete details on rotary cutting. Cut on all the marked lines, as indicated in **Diagram 3A**. Carefully press the triangle squares open, pressing the seam toward the dark fabric. Trim off the triangle points at the seam ends, as shown in **3B**. You will get eight triangle squares from each grid, which is enough for two blocks. Continue marking and cutting triangle squares until you have made the number required for the quilt size you are making.

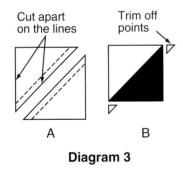

Diagram 3

Piecing the Nine-Patch Blocks

Each Nine-Patch block requires two different segment variations, as shown in **Diagram 4**. There are two A segments and one B segment in each block. The directions given here will allow you to piece three blocks at one time from the same two fabrics.

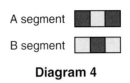

Diagram 4

Step 1. The blocks are assembled using a strip-piecing technique. Refer to the Cutting Chart to determine the total number of light and dark strips required to make the Nine-Patch blocks for your quilt. Cut the strips from an assortment of fabrics, then separate them into light and dark piles.

Step 2. Select a dark strip and a light strip from the piles. From the dark strip, cut two 10¾-inch-long pieces and one 5½-inch-long piece. From the light strip, cut one 10¾-inch piece and two 5½-inch pieces. Set the remaining pieces of strips aside.

Step 3. To make the A segments, use a ¼-inch seam to sew a dark 10¾-inch-long strip to each side of the light 10¾-inch-long strip, as shown in **Diagram 5A**. Press the seams toward the dark strips.

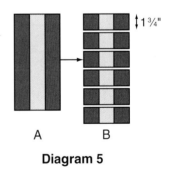

Diagram 5

Step 4. Using a rotary cutter and ruler, square up one end of the strip set. Cut 1¾-inch segments from the unit, as shown in **5B**; you should be able to cut six segments.

Step 5. To make the B segments, sew the light 5½-inch-long strips to each side of the dark 5½-inch-long strip, as shown in **Diagram 6A** on page 6. Press the seams toward the dark strip.

Step 6. Using a rotary cutter and ruler, square up one end of the strip set. Cut 1¾-inch segments from the strip set, as shown in **6B**; you should be able to cut three segments.

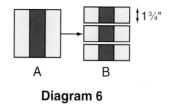

Diagram 6

Step 7. Sew two A segments and one B segment together, as shown in **Diagram 7**, matching seams carefully. Since the seam allowances are pressed in opposite directions, the intersections should fit together tightly. Stitch, using ¼-inch seam allowances. Repeat with the remaining segments.

Diagram 7

Step 8. Repeat Steps 2 through 7, piecing three Nine-Patch blocks from each pair of strips until you have completed the number of Nine-Patch blocks required for your quilt.

ASSEMBLING THE DOUBLE NINE-PATCH BLOCKS

Step 1. Lay out five small Nine-Patch blocks and four triangle squares in three rows, as shown in **Diagram 8**, making sure the triangle squares are positioned correctly. Sew the blocks into rows, pressing the seams toward the triangle squares.

Diagram 8

Step 2. Sew the rows together, matching seams carefully. Press.

Step 3. Repeat, assembling the required number of Double Nine-Patch blocks for your quilt.

ASSEMBLING THE QUILT TOP

Step 1. Use a design wall or other flat surface to lay out the Double Nine-Patch blocks, as shown in the **Quilt Diagram**. The quilt shown in the diagram is the double size, which has eight rows of six blocks each. The layout for the lap-size quilt is the same, except there are six rows of four blocks each. Pay attention to the orientation of the quilt blocks; every other block is turned 90 degrees.

Step 2. Referring to the **Assembly Diagram**, sew the blocks together in rows, pressing the seams in opposite directions from row to row. Sew the rows together, matching seams carefully. Press.

Assembly Diagram

Quilt Diagram

ADDING THE BORDERS

Step 1. For either quilt, the 2½-inch-wide black inner border strips must first be joined end to end to achieve the necessary length. For the lap-size quilt, sew two strips together for each side border. For the top and bottom borders, cut one strip in half crosswise, and sew one half to each of the two remaining full-length strips. For the double-size quilt, sew eight strips together in pairs, making four long border strips. Cut the remaining strip in half crosswise, and sew one half each to two of the long border strips.

Step 2. Add the top and bottom borders first. Measure the width of the quilt top, taking the measurement through the horizontal center of the quilt rather than along the top or bottom. Trim the two shorter black border strips to this exact length.

Step 3. Fold one trimmed strip in half crosswise and crease. Unfold it and position it right side down along the top edge of the quilt, with the crease at the vertical midpoint. Pin at the midpoint and ends first, then along the length of the entire end, easing in fullness if necessary. Sew the border to the quilt top using a ¼-inch seam allowance. Press the seam toward the border. Repeat on the bottom edge of the quilt.

Step 4. Measure the length of the quilt, taking the measurement through the vertical center of the quilt and including the top and bottom borders. Trim the remaining black border strips to this exact length.

Step 5. Fold one strip in half crosswise and crease. Unfold it and position it right side down along one side of the quilt top, matching the crease to the horizontal midpoint. Pin at the midpoint and ends first, then across the entire length of the quilt top, easing in fullness if necessary. Stitch, using a ¼-inch seam allowance. Press the seam allowance toward the border. Repeat on the opposite side of the quilt.

Step 6. In the same manner, piece together the 4½-inch-wide outer border strips to get four long borders. Measure and add the borders to the quilt top, adding the top and bottom borders first, then the side borders.

QUILTING AND FINISHING

Step 1. Mark the quilt top for quilting. The quilt shown has outline quilting in the triangle squares and a large X quilted through the center of each Nine-Patch block. A diagonal grid in the borders completes the design.

Step 2. Regardless of which quilt size you've chosen to make, the backing will have to be pieced. **Diagram 9** illustrates the two quilt backs.

To make the backing for the lap-size quilt, divide the backing fabric crosswise into two equal pieces, and trim the selvages.

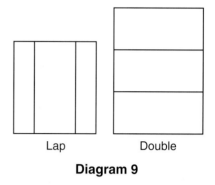

Lap   Double

Diagram 9

Step 3. Cut one of the pieces in half lengthwise, and sew one half to each side of the full-width piece. Press the seams open.

Step 4. To make the backing for the double-size quilt, divide the fabric crosswise into three equal pieces, and trim the selvages. Sew the three pieces together along the long sides, then press the seams open.

Step 5. Layer the quilt top, batting, and backing, and baste. Quilt as desired.

Step 6. Referring to the directions on page 121 in "Quiltmaking Basics," make and attach double-fold binding. To calculate the amount of binding needed for the quilt size you are making, add up the length of the four sides of the quilt and add 9 inches. The total is the approximate number of inches of binding you will need.

OKLAHOMA NINE PATCH

Color Plan

Photocopy this page and use it to experiment with color schemes for your quilt.

DOUBLE NINE PATCH

Skill Level: *Easy*

This bright and cheerful twin-size quilt comes together quickly when you use strip sets to make the small Nine-Patch blocks. Its easy construction makes this a good quilt for a beginner. More experienced quilters can have fun experimenting with the pattern: Try it as a scrap quilt for a really different look!

BEFORE YOU BEGIN

The directions for this quilt are written based on using a quick-and-easy method for making Nine-Patch blocks. Strips of fabric are sewn together into strip sets. The strip sets are then cut apart and resewn into blocks. Read through the general construction directions in "Nine-Patch Basics," beginning on page 102, for further details on this technique.

Each Double Nine-Patch block in this quilt is composed of five 4½-inch Nine-Patch blocks and four 4½-inch setting squares. The small, single Nine-Patch blocks are used again as corner squares at the intersections where the sashing strips meet.

CHOOSING FABRICS

The quiltmaker chose a blue print and a burgundy print. The two colors are close to each other in value, but are different enough in color and scale to provide interest. They both contrast well with the cream fabric.

This simple pattern could also be made with just one color be-

Quilt Sizes			
	Twin (shown)	Double	Queen
Finished Quilt Size	67½" × 103½"	85½" × 103½"	94½" × 103½"
Finished Block Size			
Double Nine Patch	13½"	13½"	13½"
Small Nine Patch	4½"	4½"	4½"
Number of Blocks			
Double Nine Patch	24	30	30
Small Nine Patch	135	170	180

Materials			
	Twin	Double	Queen
Cream	5⅜ yards	6¾ yards	7¼ yards
Blue print	1¾ yards	2⅛ yards	2¼ yards
Burgundy print	½ yard	⅝ yard	⅝ yard
Backing	6½ yards	8¼ yards	9 yards
Batting	74" × 110"	92" × 110"	101" × 110"
Binding	¾ yard	⅞ yard	⅞ yard

NOTE: *Yardages are based on 44/45-inch-wide fabrics that are at least 42 inches wide after preshrinking.*

sides the cream. Or, to change the look completely, use the pattern to make a scrap quilt. Two small Nine-Patch blocks can be cut from a pair of 8-inch-long strip sets.

To help develop your own unique color scheme for the quilt, photocopy the **Color Plan** on page 17, and use crayons or colored pencils to experiment with different color arrangements.

Cutting Chart

Fabric	Used For	Strip Width	Number of Strips		
			Twin	Double	Queen
Cream	Sashing strips	5"	13	17	21
	Setting squares	5"	12	15	15
	Strip sets	2"	28	35	36
Blue print	Strip sets	2"	28	34	36
Burgundy print	Strip sets	2"	7	9	9

CUTTING

All measurements include ¼-inch seam allowances. Referring to the Cutting Chart, cut the required number of strips in the width needed. Cut all strips across the fabric width (crosswise grain).

When cutting the cream fabric, be sure to keep the two sets of 5-inch-wide strips separated; one set is for the sashing strips, and one set is for the setting squares. To prepare the sashing strips, cut the 5-inch-wide strips into 14-inch-long rectangles. To prepare the setting squares for the Double Nine-Patch blocks, cut the 5-inch-wide strips into 5-inch squares.

Note: Cut and piece one sample block before cutting all the fabric for the quilt.

PIECING THE SMALL NINE-PATCH BLOCKS

The Double Nine-Patch block is made up of five small Nine-Patch blocks and four setting squares, as shown in the **Block Diagram.**

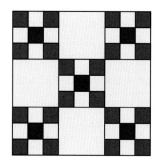

Block Diagram

Each small Nine-Patch block requires two different segment variations. The A segment is made with the blue print fabric, and the B segment is made with the burgundy print fabric, as illustrated in **Diagram 1.** The cream fabric is used in both variations.

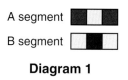

Diagram 1

Step 1. The blocks are assembled using a strip-piecing technique. Refer to the Cutting Chart to determine the total number of 2-inch strips you need to cut from each of the fabrics. Cut all strips across the width of your fabric, from selvage to selvage. The strips should be approximately 42 inches long.

Step 2. To make the A segments, use a ¼-inch seam to sew a blue print strip to each side of a cream strip, as shown in **Diagram 2.** Press the seam allowances toward the blue strips.

Diagram 2

Step 3. Using a rotary cutter and ruler, square up one end of the strip set. Refer to page 115 in "Quiltmaking Basics" for complete details on using

making strip sets and cutting them into segments until you have assembled the required number of B segments for your quilt. You need one B segment for each small Nine-Patch block in your quilt.

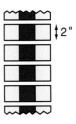

Diagram 5

Step 6. Sew two A segments and one B segment together, as shown in **Diagram 6,** matching seams carefully. Since the seam allowances on the segments are pressed in opposite directions, the intersections should fit together tightly. Stitch, using a ¼-inch seam allowance. Press. Repeat until all blocks are assembled.

Diagram 6

ASSEMBLING THE DOUBLE NINE-PATCH BLOCKS

Step 1. Lay out five small Nine-Patch blocks and four setting squares into three rows, as shown in **Diagram 7.** Sew the blocks into rows. For less bulk, press the seams toward the setting squares.

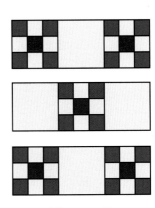

Diagram 7

a rotary cutter. Cut 2-inch-wide segments from the strip set, as shown in **Diagram 3.** You should be able to cut 20 segments. Continue making strip sets and cutting them into segments until you have assembled the required number of A segments for your quilt. You need two A segments for each small Nine-Patch block in your quilt.

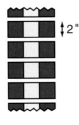

Diagram 3

Step 4. To make the B segments, sew a cream strip to each side of a burgundy strip, as shown in **Diagram 4.** Press the seams toward the burgundy strip.

Diagram 4

Step 5. Using a rotary cutter and ruler, square up one end of the strip set. Cut 2-inch-wide segments from the strip set, as shown in **Diagram 5.** You should be able to cut 20 segments. Continue

Step 2. Sew the rows together, matching seams carefully. Press.

Step 3. Repeat until you have assembled the required number of Double Nine-Patch blocks for your quilt.

ASSEMBLING THE QUILT TOP

Step 1. Use a design wall or other flat surface to lay out the Double Nine-Patch blocks, small Nine-Patch blocks, and sashing strips. Refer to the appropriate quilt diagram for the correct layout for your quilt.

Step 2. Sew the blocks and strips together into rows, pressing the seams toward the sashing strips. Sew the rows together, matching seams carefully. Press.

QUILTING AND FINISHING

Step 1. Mark the quilt top for quilting, if desired. The quilt shown has parallel diagonal lines quilted across the entire top to highlight the design created by the small Nine-Patch blocks. **Diagram 8** illustrates the quilting design.

Twin-Size Quilt Diagram

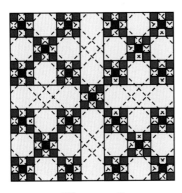

Diagram 8

Step 2. Regardless of which quilt size you have chosen to make, the backing will have to be pieced. **Diagram 9** shows the different quilt backs. To make the most efficient use of the yardage, the twin-size back is pieced with the seams running vertically. The double- and queen-size backs are pieced with the seams running horizontally.

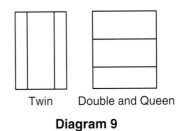

Twin   Double and Queen

Diagram 9

Double-Size Quilt Diagram

Step 3. For the twin-size quilt, cut the backing fabric crosswise into two equal segments, and trim the selvages. Cut one of the segments in half lengthwise, and sew one half to each side of the full-width piece. Press the seams open.

Step 4. For both the double- and queen-size quilts, cut the backing fabric crosswise into three equal segments, and trim the selvages. Sew two of the pieces together along the long side and press the seam open.

Step 5. Cut a piece approximately 32 inches wide from the entire length of the third piece.

Sew this strip to one side of the joined section and press.

Step 6. Layer the quilt top, batting, and backing, and baste the layers together. Quilt as desired.

Step 7. Referring to the directions on page 121 in "Quiltmaking Basics," make and attach double-fold binding. To calculate the amount of binding needed for the quilt size you are making, add up the length of the four sides of the quilt and add 9 inches. The total is the approximate number of inches of binding you will need.

Queen-Size Quilt Diagram

DOUBLE NINE PATCH

Color Plan

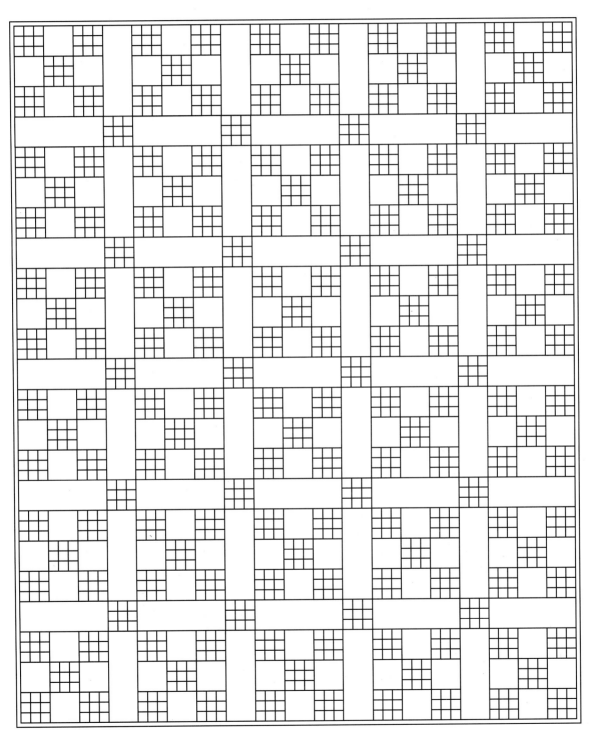

Photocopy this page and use it to experiment with color schemes for your quilt.

FOUR PATCH/NINE PATCH
Skill Level: *Easy*

*H*ere's a new twist on the typical Four-Patch/Nine-Patch pattern. Instead of Nine-Patch blocks made up of smaller Four-Patch units, this lively twin-size quilt flips the equation: Here, small Nine-Patch blocks are joined to make larger Four-Patch blocks. Additional Nine-Patch blocks form the cornerstones in the sashing.

BEFORE YOU BEGIN

Each Four-Patch block in this quilt is composed of four small Nine-Patch blocks. The blocks are joined by sashing strips, with additional Nine-Patch blocks used as cornerstones.

The directions for the Nine-Patch blocks are written based on using an easy strip-piecing technique. Strips of fabric are sewn together into strip sets. The strip sets are then cut apart and re-sewn into blocks. Read through the general construction directions in "Nine-Patch Basics," beginning on page 102, for further details on this technique.

CHOOSING FABRICS

The scrappy Nine-Patch blocks were made from a wide assortment of prints, checks, and florals. Since the directions call for narrow, $1\frac{3}{4}$-inch-wide strips to make strip sets, this is a good project for using up scraps. If you do purchase fabric for the blocks, buy small amounts of a wide variety of fabrics. Then, to tie it all together, choose a solid fabric or a subtle print such as the medium blue used here in the sashing strips and border.

To help develop your own unique color scheme for the quilt, photocopy the **Color Plan** on page 25, and use crayons or colored pencils to experiment with different color combinations.

Quilt Sizes		
	Twin (shown)	Queen
Finished Quilt Size	76" × $87\frac{1}{4}$"	$87\frac{1}{4}$" × $98\frac{1}{2}$"
Finished Block Size		
Four Patch	$7\frac{1}{2}$"	$7\frac{1}{2}$"
Nine Patch	$3\frac{3}{4}$"	$3\frac{3}{4}$"
Number of Blocks		
Four Patch	30	42
Nine Patch	162	224

Materials		
	Twin	Queen
Dark blue print	$2\frac{5}{8}$ yards	$3\frac{3}{8}$ yards
Assorted dark prints	2 yards	$2\frac{5}{8}$ yards
Assorted light prints	$1\frac{5}{8}$ yards	$2\frac{1}{4}$ yards
Navy blue	$1\frac{3}{8}$ yards	$1\frac{1}{2}$ yards
Cream print	$\frac{5}{8}$ yard	$\frac{3}{4}$ yard
Dark print	$\frac{5}{8}$ yard	$\frac{3}{4}$ yard
Backing	$5\frac{1}{2}$ yards	8 yards
Batting	84" × 94"	94" × 104"
Binding	$\frac{5}{8}$ yard	$\frac{3}{4}$ yard

NOTE: Yardages are based on 44/45-inch-wide fabrics that are at least 42 inches wide after preshrinking.

19

Cutting Chart

Fabric	Used For	Strip Width	Number of Strips	
			Twin	Queen
Dark blue print	Sashing strips	4¼"	15	20
	Third border	2½"	9	10
Assorted dark prints	Strip sets	1¾"	35	48
Assorted light prints	Strip sets	1¾"	28	39
Navy blue	Fourth border	4½"	9	10
Cream print	First border	1½"	9	10
Dark print	Second border	1½"	9	10

CUTTING

All measurements include ¼-inch seam allowances. Referring to the Cutting Chart, cut the required number of strips in the width needed. Cut all strips across the fabric width (crosswise grain).

To make the sashing strips, cut each of the 4¼-inch-wide medium blue strips into 4¼ × 8-inch rectangles.

Note: Cut and piece one sample block before cutting all the fabric for the quilt.

PIECING THE NINE-PATCH BLOCKS

Each Four-Patch block is made up of four Nine-Patch blocks, as shown in the **Block Diagram.**

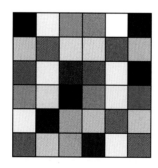

Block Diagram

Each small Nine-Patch block requires two different segment variations, as shown in **Diagram 1.** There are two A segments and one B segment in each block.

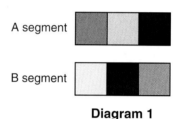

Diagram 1

Step 1. The blocks are assembled using a strip-piecing technique. Refer to the Cutting Chart to determine the total number of 1¾-inch strips required to make the Nine-Patch blocks for your quilt. Cut the correct number of light and dark strips, using an assortment of fabrics.

Step 2. To make the A segments, use a ¼-inch seam to sew a dark strip to each side of a light strip, as shown in **Diagram 2.** Press the seams toward the dark strips.

Diagram 2

Step 3. Using a rotary cutter and ruler, square up one end of the strip set. Refer to page 115 in "Quiltmaking Basics" for complete details on rotary cutting. Cut 1¾-inch-wide segments from the strip set, as shown in **Diagram 3.** You should be able to cut at least 24 segments. Continue making strip sets and cutting them into segments until you have assembled the required number of A segments needed for your quilt. You need two A segments for each Nine-Patch block.

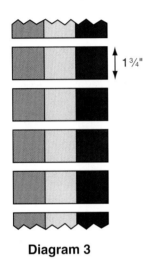

Diagram 3

Step 4. To make the B segments, sew a light strip to each side of a dark strip, as shown in **Diagram 4.** Press the seams toward the dark strip.

Diagram 4

Step 5. Using a rotary cutter and ruler, square up one end of the strip set. Cut 1¾-inch-wide seg-

ments from the strip set, as shown in **Diagram 5.** Continue making strip sets and cutting them into segments until you have assembled the required number of B segments needed for your quilt. You need one B segment for each Nine-Patch block.

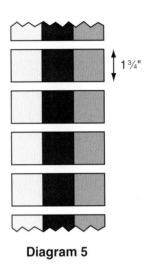

Diagram 5

Step 6. Sew two A segments and one B segment together, as shown in **Diagram 6,** matching seams carefully. Since the seam allowances on the segments are pressed in opposite directions, the intersections should fit together tightly. Stitch, using a ¼-inch seam allowance. Press. Repeat until you have assembled the required number of blocks for your quilt.

Diagram 6

ASSEMBLING THE FOUR-PATCH BLOCKS

Lay out four Nine-Patch blocks in two rows of two. Don't hesitate to flip blocks sideways or upside down to obtain a more pleasing distribution of color. When you are satisfied with the arrangement, sew the blocks together in pairs, as shown in **Diagram 7** on page 22. Press the seams in opposite directions. Sew the pairs together, as shown in the diagram. Repeat until you have assembled the number of Four-Patch blocks required for your quilt. You will have extra Nine-Patch blocks; these are used in the sashing.

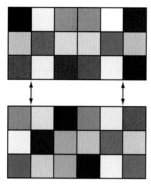

Diagram 7

ASSEMBLING THE QUILT TOP

Step 1. Use a design wall or other flat surface to lay out the Four-Patch and Nine-Patch blocks and sashing strips. Refer to the appropriate quilt diagram (on this page and page 24) for the correct layout.

Step 2. When you are satisfied with the layout, sew the blocks and sashing strips together in rows, as shown in the **Assembly Diagram**. Press the seams toward the sashing strips.

Step 3. Sew the rows together, carefully matching seams. Press the quilt top.

ADDING THE BORDERS

The borders on the quilt consist of four strips sewn together, resulting in a total finished width

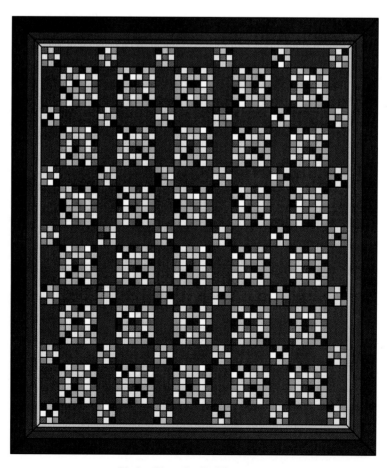

Twin-Size Quilt Diagram

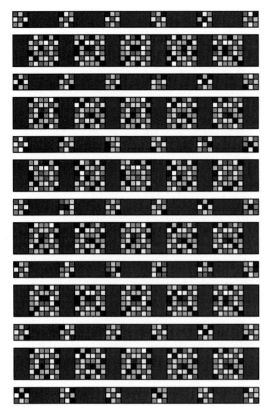

Assembly Diagram

of 8 inches. You will sew the long strips together first, then add them to the quilt top as a single unit, mitering the corners. Refer to page 119 in "Quiltmaking Basics" for complete details on adding borders with mitered corners.

Step 1. To determine the correct length for the side borders, measure the quilt top vertically through the center. To this measurement, add two times the finished width of the border (6 inches × 2) plus approximately 5 inches. This is the length you need to make the two side borders. In the same manner, measure the quilt top horizontally through the center, and calculate the length of the top and bottom borders.

Step 2. Sew the cream border strips together end to end in pairs, making four long borders. Add additional strips or parts of strips as needed to achieve the required length. Repeat for each of the three remaining borders. Be sure to keep the side border strips separate from the top and bottom border strips.

Step 3. Working with one set of side border strips, pin and sew the long strips together lengthwise in the order shown in **Diagram 8**. Press the seams toward the widest strip. Repeat with the second set of side border strips.

Diagram 8

Step 4. In the same manner, pin and sew the top and bottom border strips together into two sets. Press the seams toward the widest strip.

Step 5. Pin and sew the four borders to the quilt top. Refer to page 119 in "Quiltmaking Basics" for instructions on finishing the miters. When preparing the miters, be sure to carefully match up the various strips in adjacent borders.

QUILTING AND FINISHING

Step 1. Mark the quilt top for quilting. The quilt shown was machine quilted in an allover wavy pattern.

Step 2. Regardless of which quilt size you've chosen to make, the backing will have to be pieced. **Diagram 9** illustrates the two quilt backs.

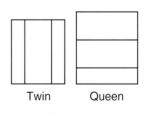

Twin   Queen

Diagram 9

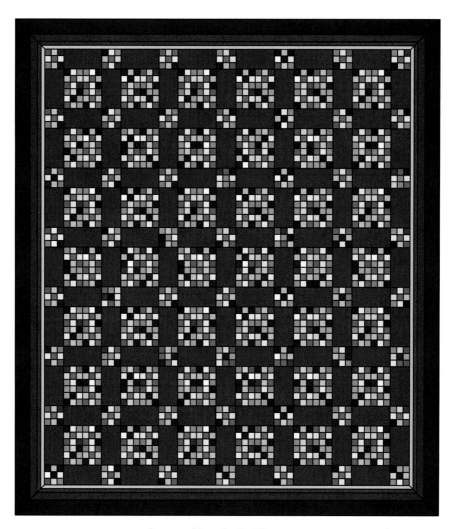

Queen-Size Quilt Diagram

To make the backing for the twin-size quilt, cut the backing fabric crosswise into two equal pieces, and trim the selvages.

Step 3. Cut one piece in half lengthwise. Sew a narrow segment to each side of the full-width segment, as shown. Press the seams open.

Step 4. To make the backing for the queen-size quilt, cut the backing fabric crosswise into three equal pieces, and trim the selvages. Sew two of the pieces together along the long side and press the seam open.

Step 5. Cut a piece that is approximately 24 inches wide from the third segment and sew it

to the long side of the joined piece. Press the seam open.

Step 6. Layer the quilt top, batting, and backing, and baste the layers together. Quilt as desired.

Step 7. Make the required length of double-fold binding for your quilt. Referring to the directions on page 121 in "Quiltmaking Basics," make and attach double-fold binding. To calculate the amount of binding needed for the quilt size you are making, add up the length of the four sides of the quilt and add 9 inches. The total is the approximate number of inches of binding you will need.

Four Patch/Nine Patch

Color Plan

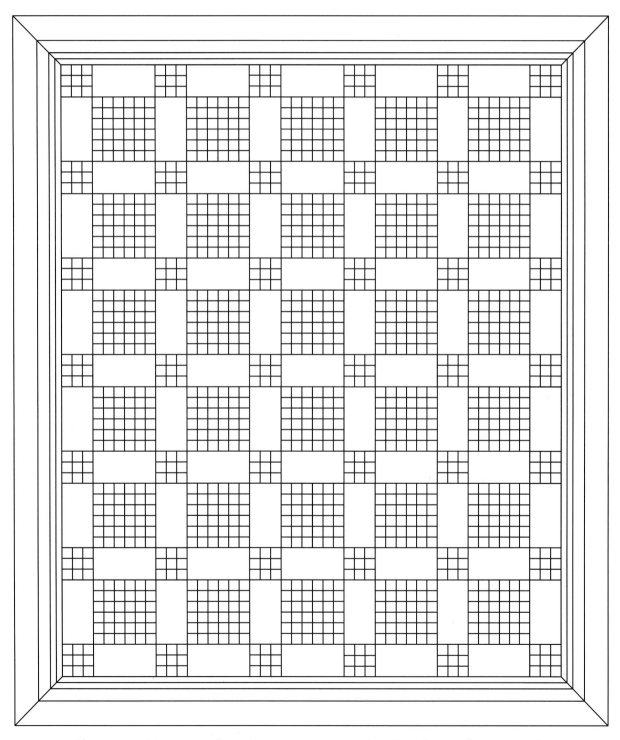

Photocopy this page and use it to experiment with color schemes for your quilt.

SNOWBALL AND NINE PATCH
Skill Level: *Easy*

*I*n this exuberant twin-size quilt, a traditional pattern gets new life through the use of scraps. The warm colors are reminiscent of autumn leaves, with a liberal sprinkling of yellow creating light and movement across the surface of the quilt. Unlike many Nine-Patch blocks, these do not follow a strict dark-light-dark pattern; the values are combined randomly. In another unique feature, the side setting triangles are topped off with scraps, making them an integral part of the quilt's design.

BEFORE YOU BEGIN

The directions for this quilt are written based on using a quick-and-easy method for making Nine-Patch blocks. Strips of fabric are sewn together into strip sets. The strip sets are then cut apart and resewn into blocks. The random-pieced borders are also made up of segments cut from the strip sets. Read through the general construction directions in "Nine-Patch Basics," beginning on page 102, for further details on this technique.

The technique used to create the Snowball blocks involves placing a small square at each corner of the larger background square, sewing them together on a diagonal, and trimming the excess from the corner. A similar technique is used to add the tips to the side setting triangles.

CHOOSING FABRICS

The scrappy Nine-Patch blocks in this quilt were made from an assortment of small-scale calico fabrics. Fabrics were repeated in the corners of the Snowball blocks and in the side setting triangles. Placement of color value is random, with lights to darks represented. As with other Nine-Patch quilts, strip piecing is used to assemble the blocks.

If you already have them, use scrap pieces of the required strip size, or purchase fat quarters or standard quarter-yard cuts of fabric. If you do purchase fabrics, the best result will be achieved by selecting a wide variety of prints in different values to get the total yardage required for your quilt. Any leftovers can be added to your stash for future scrappy projects.

Quilt Sizes		
	Twin (shown)	**Queen**
Finished Quilt Size	73½" × 83"	92½" × 102"
Finished Block Size	6¾"	6¾"
Number of Blocks		
Nine Patch	30	56
Snowball	20	42

Materials		
	Twin	**Queen**
Assorted prints	3⅛ yards	5⅛ yards
Cream	3¾ yards	5⅜ yards
Backing	5¼ yards	8⅝ yards
Batting	80" × 89"	99" × 108"

NOTE: Yardages are based on 44/45-inch-wide fabrics that are at least 42 inches wide after preshrinking.

27

Cutting Chart

Fabric	Used For	Strip Width	Number of Strips	
			Twin	Queen
Assorted prints	Strip sets and borders	2¾"	33	51
	Snowball corners and triangle tips	2¾"	7	13
Cream	Snowball blocks	7¼"	4	9
	Side setting triangles	10⅞"	2	3
	Corner setting triangles	5¾"	1	1
	Inner border	4"	6	8
	Outer border	5¼"	8	9

If you use the same fabric in two or more strip sets, be sure to combine it with different fabrics each time to help retain the scrappy flavor of this quilt.

To help develop your own unique color scheme for the quilt, photocopy the **Color Plan** on page 35, and use crayons or colored pencils to experiment with different color arrangements.

CUTTING

All measurements include ¼-inch seam allowances. Referring to the Cutting Chart, cut the required number of strips in the width needed. Cut all strips across the fabric width (crosswise grain). The number of strips called for in the Cutting Chart assumes that you will be cutting full-width (at least 42-inch-wide) fabric. If you use fat quarters or scraps, the number of strips required will vary.

To make the Snowball blocks, cut the 7¼-inch-wide strips into 7¼-inch squares. To make the corners for the Snowball blocks, cut the 2¾-inch strips into 2¾-inch squares.

To make the side setting triangles, cut the 10⅞-inch strips into 10⅞-inch squares. Referring to **Diagram 1**, cut each square diagonally both ways to get four triangles. For the corner setting triangles, cut the 5¾-inch strips into 5¾-inch squares. Cut each square in half diagonally to get two trian-

gles, as shown in the diagram. Cutting the triangles from squares in this way puts the straight grain of the fabric on the outside edge of the quilt, where it's needed for stability.

Note: Cut and piece one sample block before cutting all the fabric for the quilt.

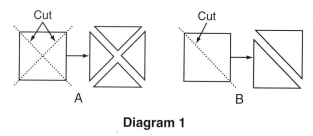

Diagram 1

PIECING THE NINE-PATCH BLOCKS

The quilt is made up of Nine-Patch blocks alternating with Snowball blocks. The **Block Diagram** illustrates the two different types of blocks. The colors shown in the diagram are just an example of what you might choose for your own quilt.

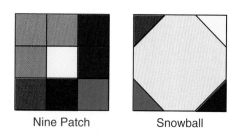

Nine Patch   Snowball

Block Diagram

Step 1. The blocks are assembled using a strip-piecing technique. Refer to the Cutting Chart to determine the total number of 2¾-inch strips you need to cut. Cut from as many different fabrics as possible, and be sure to select several color values.

Step 2. Choose three strips randomly, sewing them together lengthwise, as shown in **Diagram 2A**. Press the seams in one direction.

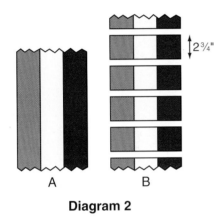

Diagram 2

Step 3. Using a rotary cutter and ruler, square up one end of the strip set, then cut it into 2¾-inch-wide segments, as shown in **2B**. See page 115 in "Quiltmaking Basics" for details on using a rotary cutter.

Step 4. Repeat Steps 2 and 3 until you have cut the required number of segments for your quilt. You will need a total of 165 segments for the twin-size quilt and 260 segments for the queen-size

quilt. These totals include both the blocks and the random-pieced borders.

Step 5. Assemble the required number of Nine-Patch blocks for your quilt. Each block contains three rows of segments, as shown in **Diagram 3**. Since seams in adjoining rows will be easier to match if pressed in opposite directions, it may be necessary to re-press some segment seams as you work. Set aside the remaining segments. They will be used later in the pieced borders.

Diagram 3

PIECING THE SNOWBALL BLOCKS

The Snowball blocks are made by sewing small squares to the corners of a larger square, then trimming the excess, creating a triangle in each corner.

Step 1. Select four different 2¾-inch squares for each Snowball block. With a pencil, lightly draw a line from corner to corner on the wrong side of each small square. Place a small square right sides together with a 7¼-inch background square, aligning the two outside edges, as shown in **Diagram 4A**.

Sew Easy

If you are using 42-inch-long strips, you may want to cut them in half crosswise before sewing them into strip sets. This will allow you to create twice as many combinations of strips, increasing the scrappy feel of the blocks.

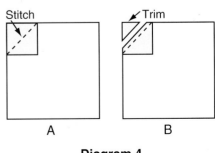

Diagram 4

Step 2. Stitch the squares together along the drawn diagonal line. Referring to **4B** on page 29, trim off the excess corner fabric, leaving a ¼-inch seam allowance.

Step 3. Open out the corner, as shown in **Diagram 5,** and press the seam allowance toward the triangle. Repeat on the three remaining corners to complete one Snowball block.

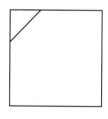

Diagram 5

Step 4. In the same manner, complete the required number of Snowball blocks for your quilt.

PREPARING THE SIDE SETTING TRIANGLES

The side setting triangles are topped with smaller triangles of scrap fabrics. The technique is similar to the one used to make the Snowball blocks.

Step 1. Select a 2¾-inch square for each triangle tip. With a pencil, lightly draw a line from corner to corner on the wrong side of each square. Align a square with the corner of a side setting triangles, as shown in **Diagram 6A.**

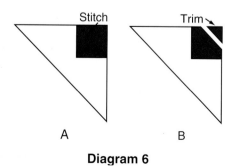

Diagram 6

Step 2. Stitch the square to the triangle along the drawn diagonal line. Trim the corner of the triangle, as shown in **6B,** leaving a ¼-inch seam allowance.

Step 3. Open out the corner, as shown in **Diagram 7,** and press the seam allowance toward the tip of the triangle. Repeat to make the required number of side setting triangles for your quilt.

Diagram 7

ASSEMBLING THE QUILT TOP

Step 1. Use a design wall or other flat surface to lay out the Nine-Patch blocks, Snowball blocks, side setting triangles, and corner setting triangles. Refer to the appropriate quilt diagram on pages 32–33 for the correct layout for your quilt.

Step 2. Referring to the **Assembly Diagram,** sew the blocks and triangles together in diagonal rows, taking care to match pieced areas of Snowball blocks with corresponding seams in adjoining Nine-Patch blocks. Press the seams away from the Nine-Patch blocks. Sew the rows together, matching seams carefully. Press.

Step 3. Sew the four corner setting triangles to the quilt top. The triangles are slightly oversize and need to be trimmed after they are added. As shown in **Diagram 8,** use your rotary cutter and ruler to

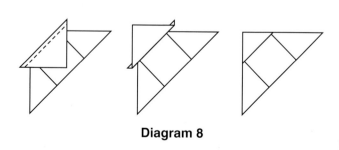

Diagram 8

Assembly Diagram

trim the triangles and square up the corners. Be sure to trim ¼ inch beyond the edge of the blocks, leaving the seam allowance intact.

MAKING AND ATTACHING THE BORDERS

The quilt has four borders. Two are pieced from the 2¾-inch-wide strip set segments left over from making the Nine-Patch blocks. The remaining two are solid borders made from the cream fabric.

Step 1. Measure the length of your quilt top, taking the measurement through the vertical center of the quilt rather than along the sides. Sew together a selection of pieced segments until you have two strips that are the required measured length.

Step 2. Fold one strip in half crosswise and crease. Unfold it and position it right side down along one side of your quilt top, with the crease at the horizontal midpoint. Pin at the midpoint and ends first, then along the length of the entire side, easing in fullness if necessary. Sew the border to the quilt top using a ¼-inch seam allowance. Repeat on the opposite side of the quilt.

Step 3. Measure the width of the quilt top, taking the measurement through the horizontal center of the quilt and including the side borders. Sew together a selection of pieced segments until you have two strips this length.

Step 4. Fold one strip in half crosswise and crease. Unfold it and position it right side down along one end of the quilt top, matching the crease to the vertical midpoint. Pin at the mid-

Twin-Size Quilt Diagram

point and ends first, then across the entire width of the quilt top, easing in fullness if necessary. Stitch, using a ¼-inch seam allowance. Repeat on the opposite end of the quilt top.

Step 5. To add the inner solid border to the twin-size quilt, sew together one and a half 4-inch-wide cream strips for each of the borders. For the queen-size quilt, join two 4-inch-wide strips for each of the borders. Measure the quilt top in the same manner as for the pieced border, and trim the strips to length. Add the side borders to the quilt first, then add the top and bottom borders.

Step 6. The second pieced border and the outer solid border are added in the same manner. Use the 5¼-inch-wide cream strips for the outer solid

border. You will again need to join strips to obtain the needed border length.

QUILTING AND FINISHING

Step 1. Mark the quilt top for quilting. The quilt shown has a feathered wreath quilted in the Snowball blocks and partial wreaths in the side and corner setting triangles. The Nine-Patch blocks are outline quilted in each square, and the solid cream borders are quilted in a cable design.

Step 2. Regardless of which quilt size you've chosen to make, the backing will have to be pieced. To make the backing for the twin-size quilt, cut the backing fabric into two equal pieces,

Queen-Size Quilt Diagram

Sew Easy

It may be necessary to add or subtract an individual 2¾-inch square to obtain the correct border length. You can also increase or decrease one or more seam allowances along the strip's length to alter the finished size slightly.

and trim the selvages. Cut one of the pieces in half lengthwise, and sew one half to each side of the full-width piece, as shown in **Diagram 9A** on page 34. Press the seams open.

Step 3. For the queen-size quilt, piece the quilt back with the seams running horizontally to make the most efficient use of the yardage. Cut the backing fabric into three equal pieces, and trim the selvages. Sew two of the pieces together along the long side, then press the seam open. Cut a 30-

inch-wide strip from the third piece, and sew it to the joined segment, as shown in **9B**.

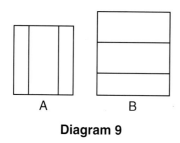

Diagram 9

Step 4. Layer the backing, batting, and quilt top, and baste. Quilt as desired.

Step 5. The edges of this quilt are finished by bringing the backing fabric around to the front side of the quilt, creating a 1½-inch-wide binding. When the quilting is complete, move the backing fabric aside and carefully trim the batting even with the quilt top. Do not cut into the backing fabric. If necessary, square up the corners and edges of the quilt top and batting. Baste ¼ inch from the edge of the quilt top on all four sides, stitching through all three layers.

Step 6. Trim the backing fabric exactly 2½ inches out from the edge on all four sides of the quilt. You may want to measure and mark the 2½-inch width before trimming it.

Step 7. Working along one side, fold the 2½ inches of backing fabric in half toward the quilt top, wrong sides together, as shown in **Diagram 10A**. The cut edge of the backing should meet the cut edge of the quilt top. Fold the backing again, bringing the folded edge to the front of the quilt, and pin it in place, as shown in **10B**.

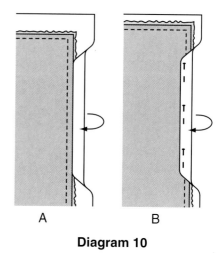

Diagram 10

Step 8. The corners are folded in the same manner as the sides. As you approach a corner along one side, continue the fold to the edge of the fabric, as shown in **Diagram 11A**. Then fold the second side, as shown in **11B**, overlapping the first and enclosing the corner.

Step 9. When the binding is completely folded and pinned in position, stitch it in place with matching thread. Don't forget to stitch the corners closed.

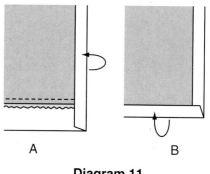

Diagram 11

Snowball and Nine Patch

Color Plan

Photocopy this page and use it to experiment with color schemes for your quilt.

MENNONITE
FOUR PATCH/NINE PATCH

Skill Level: *Easy*

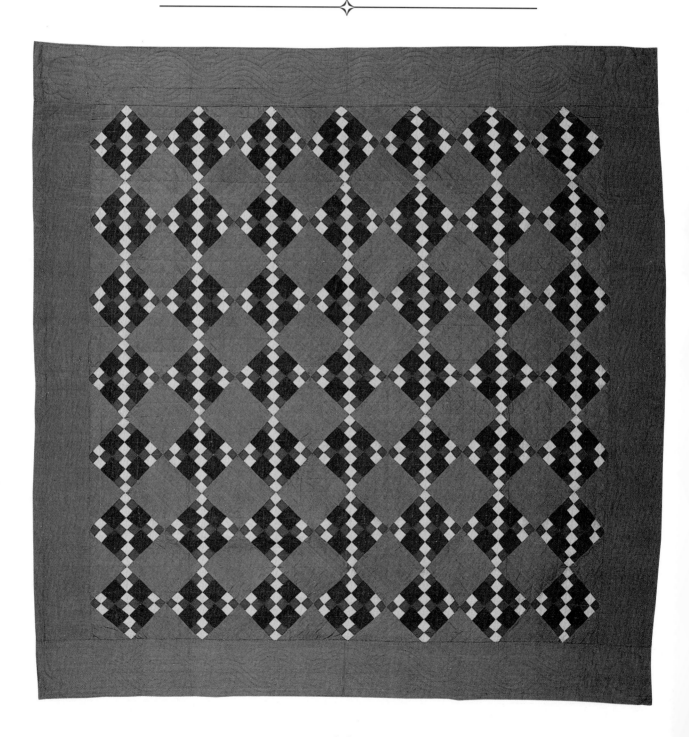

Deep, rich colors make a quiet statement in this late-nineteenth–century double-size quilt from Lancaster County, Pennsylvania. The block used is similar to a Double Nine Patch, with a simple Four-Patch block replacing the small Nine Patch. Setting the blocks on point results in a strong vertical image.

BEFORE YOU BEGIN

Each Nine-Patch block in this quilt is composed of five 2¼-inch Four-Patch blocks and four 2¼-inch setting squares. The directions for the Four-Patch blocks are written based on using a quick-and-easy piecing technique. Strips of fabric are sewn together into strip sets. The strip sets are then cut apart and re-sewn into blocks. Read through the general construction directions in "Nine-Patch Basics," beginning on page 102, for further details on this technique.

CHOOSING FABRICS

The brown, burgundy, and green solids used in this quilt are very close in value; only the gold fabric provides contrast. Such a subtle combination of colors, which is fairly common in Mennonite- and Amish-style quilts, results in a calm, quiet quilt. To achieve a similar effect in your quilt, choose solid-color fabrics in deep tones that are close in value. Or change the look by using brighter or higher-contrast colors or by substituting prints for the solids.

To help develop your own unique color scheme for the quilt, photocopy the **Color Plan** on page 43, and use crayons or colored pencils to experiment with different color arrangements.

Quilt Sizes		
	Double (shown)	Queen
Finished Quilt Size	81½" × 81½"	91" × 100½"
Finished Block Size		
Nine Patch	6¾"	6¾"
Four Patch	2¼"	2¼"
Number of Blocks		
Nine Patch	49	72
Four Patch	245	360

Materials		
	Double	Queen
Brown	4½ yards	5¾ yards
Burgundy	1⅜ yards	1¾ yards
Green	1⅛ yards	1½ yards
Gold	1⅛ yards	1½ yards
Backing	7⅞ yards	8⅝ yards
Batting	88" × 88"	97" × 107"
Binding	¾ yard	⅞ yard

NOTE: Yardages are based on 44/45-inch-wide fabrics that are at least 42 inches wide after preshrinking.

Cutting Chart

Fabric	Used For	Strip Width	Number of Strips	
			Double	Queen
Brown	Side setting triangles	10⅞"	2	3
	Borders	8"	8	9
	Setting squares	7¼"	8	12
	Corner setting triangles	5¾"	1	1
Burgundy	Setting squares	2¾"	14	20
Green	Strip sets	1⅝"	20	29
Gold	Strip sets	1⅝"	20	29

CUTTING

All measurements include ¼-inch seam allowances. Referring to the Cutting Chart, cut the required number of strips in the width needed. Cut all strips across the fabric width (crosswise grain).

To make the small setting squares for the Nine-Patch blocks, cut the 2¾-inch-wide burgundy strips into 2¾-inch squares. For the large setting squares, cut the 7¼-inch-wide brown strips into 7¼-inch squares.

The brown side setting triangles and corner setting triangles are cut from squares. To make the side setting triangles, cut the 10⅞-inch strips into 10⅞-inch squares. Cut each square diagonally both ways to get four triangles, as shown in **Diagram 1A.** To make the corner setting triangles, cut the 5¾-inch strips into 5¾-inch squares. Cut each square in half diagonally to get two triangles, as shown in **1B.** Cutting the triangles from squares in this way puts the straight grain of the fabric on the outside edge of the quilt, where it's needed for stability.

Note: Cut and piece one sample block before cutting all the fabric for the quilt.

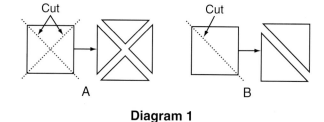

Diagram 1

PIECING THE FOUR-PATCH BLOCKS

Each Nine-Patch block is made up of five Four-Patch blocks and four setting squares, as shown in the **Block Diagram.** Strip piecing can be used to help speed up assembly of the Four-Patch blocks.

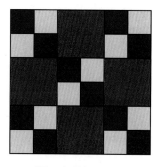

Block Diagram

Step 1. Refer to the Cutting Chart to determine the total number of 1⅝-inch strips you need to cut from the green and gold fabrics. Cut all strips across the width of the fabric, from selvage to selvage. The strips should be approximately 42 inches long.

Step 2. Place a green strip and a gold strip right sides together. Since the strips are long, you may want to pin them to keep the edges aligned. Sew them together, using a ¼-inch seam, and press the seam allowance toward the green strip. The end result will be a long strip set, as shown in **Diagram 2**.

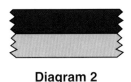

Diagram 2

Step 3. Using a rotary cutter and ruler, square up one end of the strip set. Refer to page 115 in "Quiltmaking Basics" for complete details on rotary cutting. Cut 1⅝-inch-wide segments from the strip set, as shown in **Diagram 3**. You should be able to cut at least 25 segments. Continue making strip sets and cutting them into segments until you have assembled the required number of segments for your quilt. You will need two segments for each Four-Patch block.

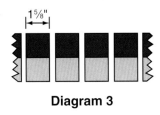

Diagram 3

Step 4. To make each Four-Patch block, lay out two segments, as shown in **Diagram 4**. Sew the segments together, carefully matching seams.

Press. Repeat, making the required number of Four-Patch blocks for your quilt.

Diagram 4

ASSEMBLING THE NINE-PATCH BLOCKS

Step 1. Lay out five Four-Patch blocks and four small setting squares, as shown in **Diagram 5**, and sew them together into rows. Press the seams toward the setting squares.

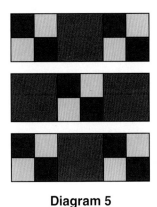

Diagram 5

Step 2. Sew the rows together, matching seams carefully. Press.

Step 3. Repeat until you have assembled the required number of Nine-Patch blocks for your size quilt.

ASSEMBLING THE QUILT TOP

Step 1. Use a design wall or other flat surface to lay out the Nine-Patch blocks, setting squares, side setting triangles, and corner setting triangles.

Refer to the appropriate quilt diagram for the correct layout for your quilt.

Step 2. Referring to the **Assembly Diagram**, sew the blocks and triangles together in diagonal rows, pressing the seams toward the setting squares and triangles. Sew the rows together, matching seams carefully.

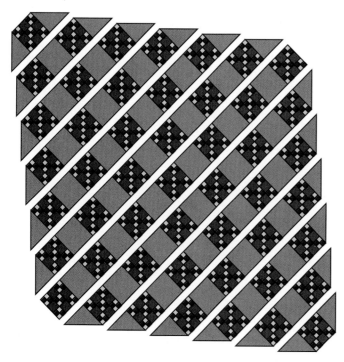

Assembly Diagram

Step 3. Sew the four corner triangles to the quilt top. The triangles are slightly oversize and need to be trimmed after they are added. Use your rotary cutter and ruler to trim the triangles and square up the corners, as shown in **Diagram 6.**

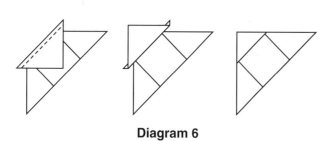

Diagram 6

ADDING THE BORDERS

The borders are sewn on in exactly the same manner for both quilts. For the queen-size quilt, you will make more efficient use of the yardage if you add the top and bottom borders first, then add the side borders. For the double-size quilt, sew the side borders on first, then add the top and bottom borders.

Step 1. For either quilt, begin by sewing the 8-inch-wide brown strips together in pairs, making four long border strips. For the queen-size quilt, cut the remaining strip in half crosswise, and sew one half each to two of the long border strips.

Step 2. For the double-size quilt, measure the length of the quilt top, taking the measurement through the vertical center of the quilt rather than along the edges. Trim two of the long border strips to this length.

Step 3. Fold one strip in half crosswise and crease. Unfold it and position it right side down along one side of the quilt top, with the crease at the midpoint. Pin at the midpoint and ends first, then along the length of the entire side, easing in fullness if necessary. Sew the border to the quilt top using a 1/4-inch seam allowance. Press the seam allowance toward the border. Repeat on the opposite side of the quilt.

Step 4. Measure the width of the quilt top, taking the measurement through the horizontal center of the quilt and including the side borders. Cut the remaining two borders to this length.

Step 5. In the same manner as for the side borders, position and pin a strip along one end of the quilt top, easing in fullness if necessary. Sew the border to the quilt top using a 1/4-inch seam allowance. Press the seam allowance toward the border. Repeat on the opposite end of the quilt.

Step 6. To add the borders to the queen-size quilt, follow the same steps, but do them in a different order. Refer to Steps 4 and 5 first, adding the top and bottom borders. Then refer to Steps 2 and 3 to add the side borders.

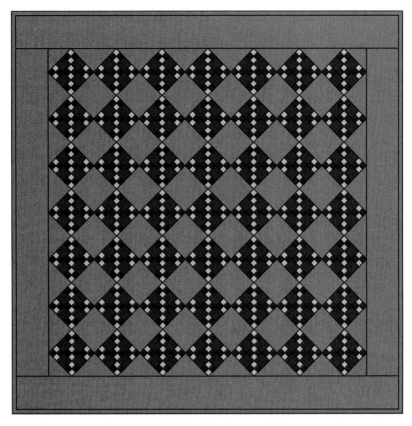

Double-Size Quilt Diagram

QUILTING AND FINISHING

Step 1. Mark the quilt top for quilting. In the quilt shown, a grid of vertical and horizontal lines in the inner quilt contrasts with the on-point position of the blocks. The borders are quilted in a cable design.

Step 2. Regardless of which quilt size you've chosen to make, the backing will have to be pieced. **Diagram 7** illustrates the two quilt backs. For both quilts, begin by cutting the backing fabric into three equal pieces and trimming the selvages.

Step 3. For the double-size quilt, cut a strip 26 inches wide from two of the pieces. Sew one of these strips to each side of the full-width panel, as shown in **7A**. Press the seams open.

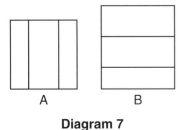

A   B

Diagram 7

— Sew Easy —

If you prefer to have a seamless quilt back, purchase extra-wide fabric at your local quilt shop or through a mail-order catalog. Quilt backing fabric is available in both 90- and 108-inch widths. This is especially useful in a case like this, where the backing for the double-size quilt needs to be just slightly larger than two widths of 44-inch-wide fabric.

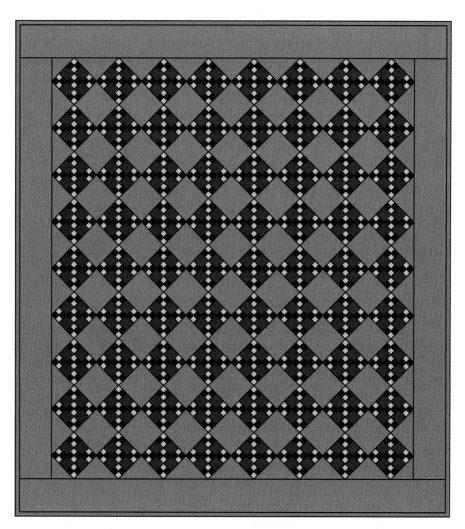

Queen-Size Quilt Diagram

Step 4. For the queen-size quilt, sew two of the pieces together along the long side. Cut a strip 29 inches wide from the third piece, and sew it to one side of the joined segment, as shown in **7B**. Press the seams open.

Step 5. Layer the quilt top, batting, and backing; baste. Quilt as desired.

Step 6. Referring to the directions on page 121 in "Quiltmaking Basics," make and attach double-fold binding. To calculate the amount of binding needed for the quilt size you are making, add up the length of the four sides of the quilt and add 9 inches. The total is the approximate number of inches of binding you will need.

MENNONITE
FOUR PATCH/NINE PATCH
Color Plan

Photocopy this page and use it to experiment with color schemes for your quilt.

DOTS AND DASHES

Skill Level: *Intermediate*

T he basic Nine-Patch block teams up with a traditional Rail-Fence block in this vibrant lap-size quilt. An assortment of red fabrics works together to unify the scraps and create terrific energy. The border is easy to piece using extra Rail-Fence blocks.

BEFORE YOU BEGIN

The directions for this quilt are written based on using an easy strip-piecing technique for making the Nine-Patch blocks. Strips of fabric are sewn together into strip sets. The strip sets are then cut apart and resewn into blocks. The Rail-Fence blocks are even easier to construct: Simply sew strips into sets, then cut the strip sets apart. No further sewing is necessary. Read through the general construction directions in "Nine-Patch Basics," beginning on page 102, for further details on strip piecing.

The outer pieced border is simply Rail-Fence blocks sewn together into long strips.

CHOOSING FABRICS

The Nine-Patch blocks in this quilt appear to be totally scrappy, but they are actually all made from the same strip sets. Flipping the segments within the blocks or turning the completed blocks in different directions adds to the illusion that many different fabrics were used. Choose four different red prints and five different light solids or prints to make these strip sets. The inner border is pieced from these same four reds, plus one or two more for variety.

The Rail-Fence blocks also are not as totally scrappy as they seem. Most of the fabric combinations appear at least four or five times and are used in both the inner quilt and the outer border. For best results, combine a wide variety of prints and solids in different values to get the total yardage required. Using full-width yardage will make construction faster and easier.

To help develop your own unique color scheme for the quilt, photocopy the **Color Plan** on page 51, and use crayons or colored pencils to experiment with different color combinations.

Quilt Sizes

	Lap (shown)	Queen
Finished Quilt Size	50¼" × 63"	83¾" × 105"
Finished Block Size	4½"	7½"
Number of Blocks		
Nine Patch	18	18
Rail Fence	96	96

Materials

	Lap	Queen
Assorted darks	1½ yards	3⅝ yards
Assorted lights	1⅛ yards	2¾ yards
Cream	1¼ yards	2 yards
Red prints	¾ yard	2 yards
Backing	3½ yards	8 yards
Batting	56" × 69"	90" × 111"
Binding	½ yard	¾ yard

NOTE: Yardages are based on 44/45-inch-wide fabrics that are at least 42 inches wide after preshrinking.

Cutting Chart

Fabric	Used For	Lap		Queen	
		Strip Width	Number of Strips	Strip Width	Number of Strips
Assorted darks	Strip sets	2"	24	3"	40
Assorted lights	Strip sets	2"	17	3"	30
Cream	Setting squares	5"	3	8"	4
	Side setting triangles	7⅝"	2	11⅞"	2
	Corner setting triangles	4⅛"	1	6¼"	1
Red prints	Inner border	2"	5	3"	9
	Strip sets	2"	4	3"	8

CUTTING

All measurements include ¼-inch seam allowances. Referring to the Cutting Chart, cut the required number of strips in the width needed. Cut all strips across the fabric width (crosswise grain). The number of strips called for in the Cutting Chart assumes that you will be cutting full-width (at least 42-inch-wide) fabric. If you use fat quarters or scraps, the number of strips required will vary.

The side setting triangles and corner setting triangles are cut from squares. To make the side setting triangles, cut the 7⅝-inch-wide strips into 7⅝-inch squares (11⅞-inch strips and squares for the queen size). Cut each square diagonally both ways to get four triangles, as shown in **Diagram 1A.** To make the corner setting triangles, cut the 4⅛-inch-wide strip into 4⅛-inch squares (6¼-inch strips and squares for the queen size). Cut each square in half diagonally to get two triangles, as shown in **1B.** Cutting the triangles from squares in this way puts the straight grain of the fabric on the outside edge of the quilt, where it's needed for stability.

Note: Cut and piece one sample block before cutting all the fabric for the quilt.

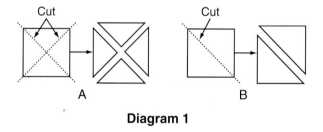

Diagram 1

PIECING THE BLOCKS

This quilt is made up of two different pieced blocks, as shown in the **Block Diagram.** Solid setting squares, side setting triangles, and corner setting triangles complete the inner quilt.

Both the Nine-Patch blocks and the Rail-Fence blocks are assembled using easy strip-piecing techniques. Additional Rail-Fence blocks are used to make the outer pieced border.

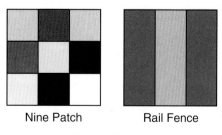

Nine Patch   Rail Fence

Block Diagram

Piecing the Nine-Patch Blocks

Each Nine-Patch block requires two different segment variations, as shown in **Diagram 2**. There are two A segments and one B segment in each block.

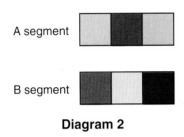

A segment

B segment

Diagram 2

Step 1. The blocks are assembled using a strip-piecing technique. Refer to the Cutting Chart to determine the total number of strips required to make the Nine-Patch blocks for your quilt. Be sure to cut strips in the correct width for the quilt size you are making. Cut the correct number of red and light strips from an assortment of fabrics.

Step 2. To make the A segments, use a ¼-inch seam to sew a light strip to each side of a red strip, as shown in **Diagram 3A**. Press the seams toward the red strip.

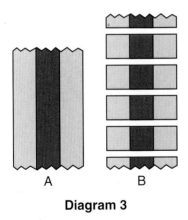

A   B

Diagram 3

Step 3. Using a rotary cutter and ruler, square up one end of the strip set. See page 115 in "Quiltmaking Basics" for complete details on rotary cutting. Cut segments from the strip set, as shown in **3B**. For the lap-size quilt, cut 2-inch-wide segments; for the queen-size quilt, cut

3-inch-wide segments. Continue making strip sets and cutting them into segments until you have assembled the required number of A segments needed for your quilt. You need two A segments for each Nine-Patch block in your quilt.

Step 4. To make the B segments, sew a different red print strip to each side of a light strip, as shown in **Diagram 4A**. Press the seams toward the red print strips.

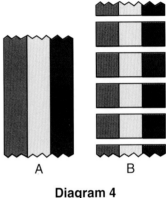

A   B

Diagram 4

Step 5. Using a rotary cutter and ruler, square up one end of the strip set. Cut segments from the strip set, as shown in **4B**. For the lap-size quilt, cut 2-inch-wide segments; for the queen-size quilt, cut 3-inch-wide segments. Continue making strip sets and cutting them into segments until you have assembled the required number of B segments needed for the quilt size you are making. You need one B segment for each Nine-Patch block in your quilt.

Step 6. Sew two A segments and one B segment together, as shown in **Diagram 5** on page 48, matching seams carefully. To keep the blocks as scrappy looking as possible, alter the fabric placement by flipping some segments end for end before joining them. Since the seam allowances on the segments are pressed in opposite directions, the intersections should fit together tightly. Stitch, using a ¼-inch seam allowance. Press. Repeat until you have assembled the required number of blocks for your quilt.

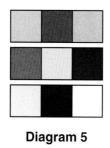

Diagram 5

Piecing the Rail-Fence Blocks

The scrappy Rail-Fence blocks can also be assembled by strip piecing. Each block is sewn from two dark strips and one light strip.

Step 1. Sew a different dark strip to each side of a light strip, as shown in **Diagram 6A.** Press the seams toward the dark strips.

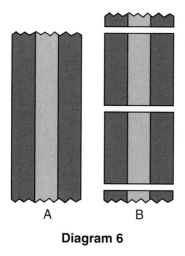

A   B

Diagram 6

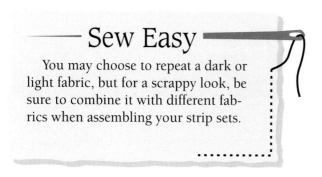

Sew Easy

You may choose to repeat a dark or light fabric, but for a scrappy look, be sure to combine it with different fabrics when assembling your strip sets.

Step 2. Using a rotary cutter and ruler, square up one end of the strip set. Cut segments from the strip set, as shown in **6B.** Cut 5-inch segments for the lap-size quilt and 8-inch segments for the queen-size quilt. Continue making strip sets and cutting them into segments until you have the required number of Rail-Fence blocks for your quilt.

Assembling the Quilt Top

Step 1. The blocks in this quilt are set on point. Use a design wall or flat surface to arrange blocks and side setting triangles in diagonal rows, as shown in the **Assembly Diagram.** The diagram illustrates the lap-size quilt. Except for the number of blocks, the layout for the queen-size quilt is the same.

Step 2. When you are satisfied with the layout, sew the blocks into rows. Press the seams in each row in the same direction. Press seams in adjoining rows in opposite directions. Sew the rows together, matching seams carefully. Press.

Step 3. Add the corner triangles. The triangles are slightly oversize and need to be trimmed after they are added. Press the seams toward the triangles, then use your rotary cutter to trim the triangles and square up the corners. Be sure to trim ¼ inch beyond the edge of the blocks, leaving the seam allowance intact.

Adding the Inner Border

Step 1. The inner border is pieced from the same red fabrics used for the blocks. You can use one fabric on all four sides of the quilt, use a different fabric on each side, or use several different fabrics on each side. Piece together red strips to make two long borders. Measure the length of the quilt top, taking the measurement through the vertical center of the quilt rather than along the sides. Trim strips to the exact measured length.

Step 2. Fold one strip in half crosswise and crease. Unfold it and position it right side down along one side of the quilt top, with the crease at the horizontal midpoint. Pin at the midpoint and ends first, then along the length of the entire side,

Assembly Diagram

easing in fullness if necessary. Sew the border to the quilt top using a ¼-inch seam allowance. Repeat on the opposite side of the quilt.

Step 3. Piece together red strips to make two long borders. Measure the width of the quilt top, taking the measurement through the horizontal center of the quilt and including the side borders. Trim the strips to the exact measured length.

Step 4. Fold one strip in half crosswise and crease. Unfold it and position it right side down along one end of the quilt top, matching the crease to the vertical midpoint. Pin at the midpoint and ends first, then across the entire width of the quilt top, easing in fullness if necessary. Stitch, using a ¼-inch seam allowance. Repeat on the opposite end of the quilt top.

ADDING THE OUTER BORDER

Step 1. The outer pieced border is made up of Rail-Fence blocks. Place the quilt top on a design

wall or other flat surface, then position the blocks for the pieced border around the quilt top. Move the blocks around until you are satisfied with the arrangement.

Note: In the quilt shown in the **Quilt Diagram** on page 50 and in the photo on page 44, the orientation is changed for two of the blocks in the border. This does not change the manner in which the borders are pieced and added; simply remember to turn one block at one end of the top and bottom borders.

Step 2. Measure the length of the quilt top in the same manner as for the inner border. Join Rail-Fence blocks until you have a side border strip of the required length. It may be necessary to add or remove individual strips to make the border fit. Press all the seams in the same direction. Repeat to make a second side border strip.

Step 3. Pin and sew a border to one side of your quilt as you did with the inner border, easing in fullness as necessary. Repeat on the opposite side of the quilt.

Step 4. Measure the width of the quilt top in the same manner as for the inner border. Sew Rail-Fence blocks together until you have obtained the measured length. If needed, add or remove individual strips to make the border fit. Press the seams in one direction. Repeat to make a second strip.

Step 5. In the same manner as for the inner border, pin and sew a pieced strip to one end of your quilt, easing in fullness as necessary. Repeat on the opposite end of the quilt.

QUILTING AND FINISHING

Step 1. Mark the top for quilting. The quilt shown has a 1-inch horizontal and vertical grid stitched in the inner quilt and a 2-inch diagonal grid stitched in the borders.

Step 2. Regardless of which quilt size you are making, the backing will have to be pieced. For both sizes, you'll make the most efficient use of the yardage by running the seams horizontally across the quilt. **Diagram 7** illustrates the two quilt backs. To make the backing for the lap-size quilt, cut the yardage in half crosswise, and trim the selvages. Cut one of the pieces in half lengthwise and sew one half to each side of the full-width piece. Press the seams open.

Step 3. To make the backing for the queen-size quilt, cut the backing fabric crosswise into three equal pieces, and trim the selvages. Sew the three pieces together along the long sides and press the seams open.

Step 4. Layer the quilt top, batting, and backing; baste the layers together. Quilt as desired.

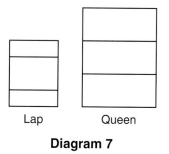

Lap   Queen

Diagram 7

Step 5. Referring to the directions on page 121 in "Quiltmaking Basics," make and attach double-fold binding. To calculate the amount of binding needed for the quilt size you are making, add up the length of the four sides of the quilt and add 9 inches. The total is the approximate number of inches of binding you will need.

Quilt Diagram

DOTS AND DASHES

Color Plan

Photocopy this page and use it to experiment with color schemes for your quilt.

51

WILD GEESE

Skill Level: *Easy*

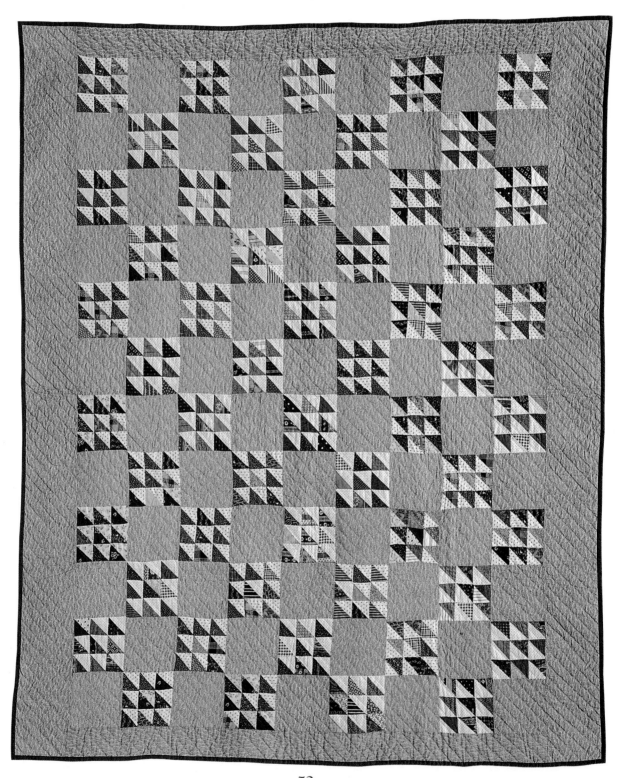

This lovely old twin-size quilt is a showcase of fabrics that were popular in the mid-1800s. The dark scraps are a myriad of colors and prints, while the lights are primarily small-scale prints and "shirtings." At first glance, the fabric in the alternating blocks gives the impression of being a mellow brown print. When you look closely, however, what you see is a very unusual mill engraving of a pink-and-green "sea foam" pattern.

BEFORE YOU BEGIN

Each Nine-Patch block is composed of nine triangle squares. The directions for making the triangle squares are based on using the grid method. You will cut 10-inch strips into squares, layer two squares together, then mark and cut the grid as directed. Each grid will result in 18 triangle squares. To get the greatest variety of triangle squares, be sure to mix and match the 10-inch fabric squares.

CHOOSING FABRICS

Making this quilt is a great way to use up some of those scraps that may be accumulating in your sewing basket. The directions call for 10-inch squares for the grid method. You could also use smaller scraps to make individual triangle squares. If you purchase fabrics, buy small amounts of each of them, particularly the dark prints. The light triangles can be the same print or several different prints. The fabric used for setting squares and borders is a subtle pink-and-green print.

If you want to make a quilt that closely resembles the one shown here, look in your local quilt shop for some of the wonderful reproduction prints that are now available. Mid-nineteenth–century fabrics are well represented among these new fabric lines.

To help develop your own unique color scheme for the quilt, photocopy the **Color Plan** on

Quilt Sizes

	Twin (shown)	Double	Queen
Finished Quilt Size	66" × 78"	84" × 102"	90" × 102"
Finished Block Size	6"	6"	6"
Number of Blocks			
Triangle squares	486	864	936
Nine-Patch blocks	54	96	104

Materials

	Twin	Double	Queen
Pink-and-green print	3 yards	4½ yards	4⅞ yards
Assorted light fabrics	2¼ yards	3⅝ yards	3⅞ yards
Assorted dark fabrics	2¼ yards	3⅝ yards	3⅞ yards
Backing	5 yards	8 yards	8⅝ yards
Batting	72" × 84"	90" × 108"	96" × 108"
Binding	⅝ yard	¾ yard	¾ yard

NOTE: *Yardages are based on 44/45-inch-wide fabrics that are at least 42 inches wide after preshrinking.*

Cutting Chart

Fabric	Used For	Strip Width	Number of Strips		
			Twin	Double	Queen
Pink-and-green print	Side borders	6½"	4	5	5
	Top and bottom borders	3½"	4	4	4
	Setting squares	6½"	9	16	18
Lights	Triangle squares	10"	7	12	13
Darks	Triangle squares	10"	7	12	13

page 59, and use crayons or colored pencils to experiment with different color arrangements.

Light and dark yardages shown for blocks are generous estimates of the total yardage actually used in the quilt. Since small amounts of many fabrics are a key ingredient for a successful scrap quilt, you will likely begin with more yardage than indicated, but not all of it will be used.

CUTTING

All measurements include ¼-inch seam allowances. Referring to the Cutting Chart, cut the required number of strips in the width needed. Cut all strips across the fabric width.

Cut the light and dark fabrics for the triangle squares into 10-inch strips, then cut the strips into 10-inch squares. For the greatest variety, cut one strip each from an assortment of fabrics. Pair up one light and one dark square for each grid of triangle squares. Be sure to mix and match the squares.

If you prefer, cut individual 2⅞-inch squares from light and dark scrap fabrics. Sort them into pairs, then mark and sew them the same way as for the grid. You will get two triangle squares from each pair of 2⅞-inch squares.

For the setting squares, cut the 6½-inch-wide strips into 6½-inch squares.

MAKING THE TRIANGLE SQUARES

Each Nine-Patch block in the quilt is composed of nine triangle squares, as shown in the **Block Diagram**. Using the easy grid method and an assortment of fabrics, make all the triangle squares first, then mix and match them, rearranging them into blocks.

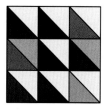

Block Diagram

Step 1. Select one light and one dark 10-inch square, and place them right sides together. Use a pencil or permanent marker to draw a grid of nine 2⅞-inch squares on the wrong side of the light fabric, as shown in **Diagram 1A**. Draw the grid so that it is at least ½ inch from the raw edges of the fabric. Referring to **1B**, carefully draw a diagonal line through each square in the grid.

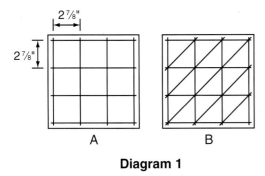

Diagram 1

Sew Easy

A fine-point permanent marker is a good choice for marking grids to make triangle squares. Even a ballpoint pen works well. Don't worry about dark ink lines causing problems in your quilt because you will be cutting the grid apart on these lines anyway. Very little ink will remain on the fabric. Choose a marker that moves easily on the fabric; pressing too hard or dragging across the grain too heavily can distort the fabric.

Step 2. Using a ¼-inch seam allowance, stitch along both sides of the diagonal lines, as shown in **Diagram 2**. Use the edge of your presser foot as a ¼-inch guide, or draw a line ¼ inch on each side of the diagonal line.

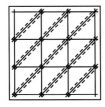

Diagram 2

Step 3. Use a rotary cutter and ruler to cut the grid apart. Refer to page 115 in "Quiltmaking Basics" for complete details on rotary cutting. Cut on all of the marked lines, as indicated in **Diagram 3A**. Carefully press the triangle squares open, pressing the seam toward the dark fabric. Trim off the triangle points at the seam ends, as shown in **3B**. You will get 18 triangle squares from each grid. Repeat with all remaining 10-inch squares.

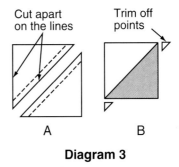

Diagram 3

ASSEMBLING THE NINE-PATCH BLOCKS

Step 1. Lay out nine triangle squares, all positioned so that the dark triangles point in the same direction. Make sure you have a good assortment of fabrics represented. Sew the squares together into rows of three, as shown in **Diagram 4**. Press the seam allowances in opposite directions from row to row. Join the rows.

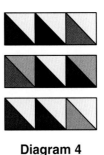

Diagram 4

Step 2. Repeat with the remaining triangle squares, making the number of blocks required for your quilt.

ASSEMBLING THE QUILT TOP

Step 1. Use a design wall or flat surface to lay out your Nine-Patch blocks and setting squares in a pleasing arrangement. Refer to the photo on page 52 and the **Quilt Diagram** when laying out the blocks. Notice that in the original quilt, the blocks in six of the vertical rows have the dark triangles in the lower left of the block. In the remaining three rows, the dark triangles are in the upper right side of the blocks. It's impossible to know whether the quiltmaker intended this difference or simply turned the rows upside down by mistake. You can decide for yourself whether you like the effect or prefer to have all the triangles in the same position.

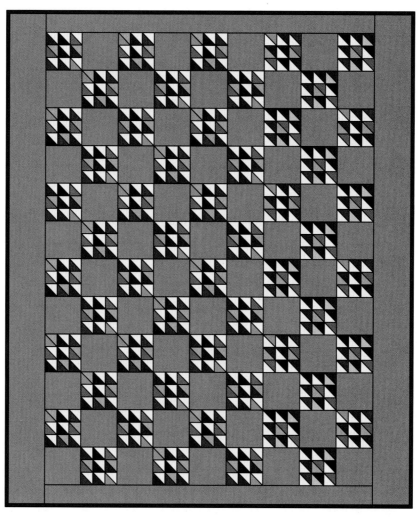

Quilt Diagram

The quilt shown in the diagram is the twin-size quilt; it consists of 12 horizontal rows with 9 blocks in each row. The layout for the other two quilts is the same, except that the double quilt has 16 horizontal rows with 12 blocks in each row, and the queen-size quilt has 16 horizontal rows with 13 blocks in each row.

Step 2. When you are satisfied with the appearance of the quilt top, sew the blocks into vertical or horizontal rows. Press the seams in each row toward the setting squares.

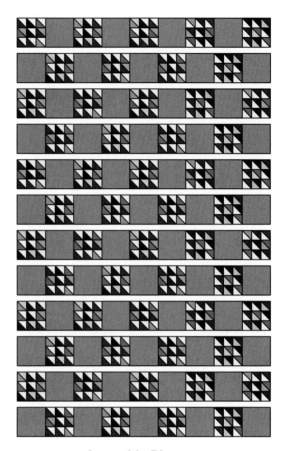

Assembly Diagram

Sew Easy

The seams will be less bulky if they are pressed toward the setting squares. If you've chosen a fabric for the setting squares that's extremely light in color, then either press the seams toward the Nine-Patch blocks or trim the seam of the Nine-Patch block so that it's narrower than the seam of the setting square.

Step 3. As shown in the **Assembly Diagram**, sew the rows together, matching seams. If you've consistently pressed all seams toward the setting squares, they should butt against each other nicely, helping you to achieve a perfect fit. Press the seams where the rows were joined.

ADDING THE BORDERS

Step 1. To add the top and bottom borders, begin by joining the 3½-inch-wide border strips in pairs to make two long borders. Measure the width of your quilt top, taking the measurement through the horizontal center of the quilt rather than along the top or bottom. Cut the two long strips to this exact length.

Step 2. Fold one strip in half crosswise and crease. Unfold it and position it right side down along one end of your quilt top, with the crease at the vertical midpoint. Pin at the midpoint and ends first, then along the length of the entire end, easing in fullness if necessary. Sew the border to the quilt top using a ¼-inch seam allowance. Repeat on the opposite end of the quilt.

Step 3. To add the side borders, first join the 6½-inch-wide border strips in pairs to make two long borders. For the double- and queen-size quilts, cut the fifth strip in half crosswise, and sew one half to each of the two long borders. Measure the length of the quilt, taking the measurement through the vertical center of the quilt and including the top and bottom borders. Trim the two border strips to this exact length.

Step 4. Fold one strip in half crosswise and crease. Unfold it and position it right side down along one side of the quilt top, matching the crease to the horizontal midpoint. Pin at the mid-point and ends first, then along the entire length of the quilt top, easing in fullness if necessary. Stitch, using a ¼-inch seam allowance. Repeat on the opposite side of the quilt top.

QUILTING AND FINISHING

Step 1. Mark the quilt top for quilting. The quilt shown was quilted with diagonal lines spaced 1 inch apart.

Step 2. Regardless of which quilt size you've chosen to make, the backing will have to be pieced. **Diagram 5** illustrates the different quilt backs. To make the backing for the twin-size quilt, cut the backing fabric into two equal pieces, and trim the selvages. Cut one of the pieces in half lengthwise, and sew one half to each side of the full-width piece. Press the seams open.

Step 3. To make the backing for the double- or queen-size quilt, cut the fabric into three equal

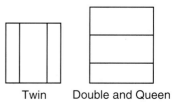

Twin   Double and Queen

Diagram 5

pieces, and trim the selvages. Sew two of the pieces together along the long side, and press the seam open. Cut a 30-inch-wide strip from the third piece, and sew it to the joined segment. Press the seam open.

Step 4. Layer the quilt top, batting, and backing, and baste the layers together. Quilt as desired.

Step 5. Referring to the directions on page 121 in "Quiltmaking Basics," make and attach double-fold binding. To calculate the amount of binding needed for the quilt size you are making, add up the length of the four sides of the quilt and add 9 inches. The total is the approximate number of inches of binding you will need.

WILD GEESE
Color Plan

Photocopy this page and use it to experiment with color schemes for your quilt.

SUMMER'S END
Skill Level: *Intermediate*

*A*lthough it's composed of basic Nine-Patch blocks in a classic Straight Furrows setting, this vibrant quilt comes alive through the masterful use of color. Made as a fun end-of-summer project using fabric purchased at summer sales, the twin-size quilt's focal point is a bold madras plaid used in the border and as one half of the triangle squares. The fabrics used in the Nine-Patch blocks and the other half of the triangle squares echo the many colors in the plaid, resulting in a complex yet harmonious burst of color.

BEFORE YOU BEGIN

The directions for this quilt are written based on using an easy strip-piecing technique for making the Nine-Patch blocks. Strips of fabric are sewn together into strip sets. The strip sets are then cut apart and resewn into blocks. Read through the general construction directions in "Nine-Patch Basics," beginning on page 102, for further details on strip piecing.

The directions for making the triangle squares call for layering two squares of fabric and stitching them together on the diagonal. The squares are then cut apart on the diagonal, resulting in two triangle squares.

CHOOSING FABRICS

To re-create the look of this quilt, you'll need to select your fabrics very carefully. In fact, we've given this quilt an Intermediate skill rating simply because of the challenge presented by coordinating the fabrics as successfully as this quiltmaker has done.

First, choose a gorgeous plaid—one with a wide range of colors. The plaid is used in the border as well as in the dark half of the triangle squares.

Next, select the prints and solids for the Nine-Patch blocks.

Quilt Sizes

	Twin (shown)	Double	Queen
Quilt Size	78" × 90"	84" × 102"	90" × 102"
Finished Block Size	6"	6"	6"
Number of Blocks			
Nine Patch	71	90	97
Triangle Squares	72	90	98

Materials

	Twin	Double	Queen
Dark plaid	3 yards	3¾ yards	4 yards
Assorted lights	2¾ yards	3⅜ yards	3⅝ yards
Assorted darks	2¾ yards	3⅜ yards	3⅝ yards
Light hand-dyed fabric	1⅛ yards	1¼ yards	2 yards
Backing	7½ yards	7⅞ yards	8⅝ yards
Batting	84" × 96"	90" × 108"	96" × 108"
Binding	¾ yard	⅞ yard	⅞ yard

NOTE: *Yardages are based on 44/45-inch-wide fabric that is at least 42 inches wide after preshrinking.*

Cutting Chart

Fabric	Used For	Strip Width	Number of Strips		
			Twin	Double	Queen
Dark plaid	Triangle squares	6⅞"	6	8	9
	Border	6½"	9	10	10
Assorted lights	Strip sets	2½"	36	45	49
Assorted darks	Strip sets	2½"	36	45	49
Light hand-dyed fabric	Triangle squares	6⅞"	6	8	9

While there are many different colors used in the quilt, each individual Nine-Patch block is made from two different values of the same color. In some blocks the fabrics are very close in value, while in others they have greater contrast. You'll need a selection of light and dark fabrics to create the distinct light and dark rows. For best results, choose small amounts of a wide variety of fabrics in colors that complement the plaid.

Finally, select a fabric for the light half of the triangle squares. The quiltmaker used a hand-dyed fabric with muted splashes of color that repeat those found in the plaid, but in pastel tones. You can choose a similar hand-dyed fabric or substitute one of the new commercial prints that resemble hand-dyed fabric.

To help develop your own unique color scheme for the quilt, photocopy the **Color Plan** on page 67, and use crayons or colored pencils to experiment with different color combinations.

The light and dark yardages shown are generous estimates of the total yardage actually used in the quilt. Since small amounts of many different fabrics are key here, you will likely begin with more yardage than indicated, but not all of it will be used.

CUTTING

All measurements include ¼-inch seam allowances. Referring to the Cutting Chart, cut the required number of strips in the width needed. Cut

Sew Easy

The piecing instructions for the Nine-Patch blocks make it easy to take advantage of scraps you have on hand. For example, two 8-inch squares in contrasting shades will yield two Nine-Patch blocks.

all strips across the fabric width (crosswise grain).

The number of strips required is based on using full-width fabric (at least 42 inches wide). If you use shorter strips, either to obtain greater variety or to use up scraps, the number of strips required will vary.

Cut the plaid and the hand-dyed fabric for the triangle squares into 6⅞-inch-wide strips, then cut the strips into 6⅞-inch squares. Pair up a square of each fabric for each pair of triangle squares.

Note: Cut and piece one sample block before cutting all the fabric for the quilt.

PIECING THE BLOCKS

In this quilt, Nine-Patch blocks alternate with triangle squares. The blocks are illustrated in the **Block Diagram.** There are two variations of the Nine-Patch blocks; the difference between them lies in the placement of the light and dark fabrics. The Nine-Patch blocks are assembled using easy strip-piecing techniques. The method used to make the triangle squares eliminates the need to cut individual triangles.

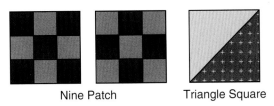

Nine Patch   Triangle Square

Block Diagram

Making the Triangle Squares

Step 1. Working on the wrong side of a 6⅞-inch square of hand-dyed fabric, use a pencil or permanent marker to draw a diagonal line from corner to corner, as shown in **Diagram 1A.**

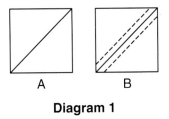

A   B

Diagram 1

Step 2. Position the marked square right sides together with a plaid square. Using a ¼-inch seam allowance, stitch along both sides of the diagonal line, as shown in **1B.** Use the edge of your presser foot as a ¼-inch guide, or draw a line ¼ inch from each side of the diagonal line.

Step 3. Using a rotary cutter and ruler, cut the squares apart on the diagonal line, as shown in **Diagram 2A.** See page 115 in "Quiltmaking Basics" for complete details on rotary cutting. Carefully press the triangle squares open, pressing the seam toward the plaid fabric. Trim off the triangle points at the seam ends, as shown in **2B.** You will get two triangle squares from each pair of squares cut in this manner. Continue marking and

cutting triangle squares until you have made the number required for the quilt size you are making.

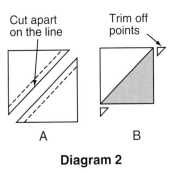

Cut apart on the line   Trim off points

A   B

Diagram 2

Piecing the Nine-Patch Blocks

Each Nine-Patch block requires two different segment variations, as shown in **Diagram 3.** One block variation uses two A segments and one B segment, while the other variation uses two B segments and one A segment. Following these directions, you'll cut three each of the two different segments—enough to assemble two blocks. When the blocks are later combined with others in the quilt top, their similarity won't be noticeable, keeping the scrappy look of your quilt intact.

A segment

B segment

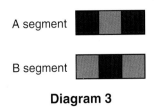

Diagram 3

Step 1. The blocks are assembled using a strip-piecing technique. Referring to the Cutting Chart, cut the total number of strips required to make the Nine-Patch blocks for your quilt. Select a pair of cut strips of different value, and cut three 2½ × 8-inch strips from each. Keep in mind that you'll need blocks that are distinctly light and blocks that are distinctly dark in order to create the effect of light and dark rows.

Step 2. Sew a dark 8-inch strip to each side of a light 8-inch strip, as shown in **Diagram 4A** on page 64. Press the seams toward the dark strips.

Step 3. Use your rotary cutter to square up one end of the sewn unit, then cut three 2½-inch-wide segments from it, as shown in **4B**.

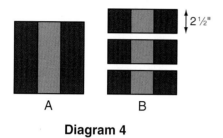

Diagram 4

Step 4. Sew a light 8-inch strip to each side of a dark 8-inch strip, as shown in **Diagram 5A**. Press the seams toward the dark strip.

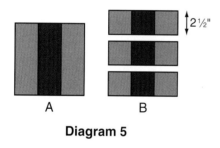

Diagram 5

Step 5. Use your rotary cutter to square up one end of the sewn unit, then cut three 2½-inch-wide segments from it, as shown in **5B**.

Step 6. Referring to the **Block Diagram** on page 63 for correct placement, position your sewn segments into three rows for each block. Sew the blocks together, matching seams carefully. Since the seam allowances on the segments are pressed in opposite directions, the intersections should fit together tightly. Stitch, using a ¼-inch seam allowance. Press.

Step 7. Repeat Steps 1 through 6 with other fabric combinations until you have assembled enough light and dark blocks for your quilt.

ASSEMBLING THE QUILT TOP

Step 1. Use a design wall or other flat surface to lay out the blocks, referring to the **Quilt Diagram**

for the correct layout. The quilt shown in the diagram is the twin-size quilt, which has 13 rows of 11 blocks each. The layout for the double- and queen-size quilts is the same, except that the double size has 15 rows of 12 blocks each, and the queen size has 15 rows of 13 blocks each. When placing blocks, make sure the light half of each triangle square is positioned against a light Nine-Patch block and the dark half is positioned against a dark Nine-Patch block.

Step 2. When you are satisfied with the layout, sew the blocks together in rows, as shown in the **Assembly Diagram**. Press the seams in opposite directions from row to row.

Step 3. Sew the rows together, carefully matching seams where blocks meet. If you've

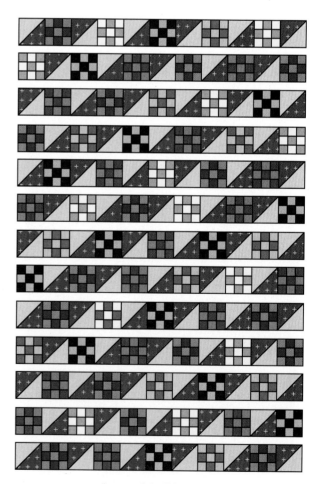

Assembly Diagram

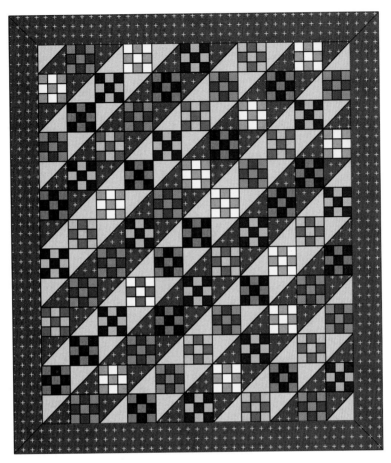

Quilt Diagram

pressed the seam allowances in opposite directions, the seams should fit tightly against each other, helping you to achieve a perfect match. Press seam allowances where rows were joined.

Sew Easy

If you have a scrap piece of fabric that's perfect for your quilt but too small for strip piecing, simply assemble the block piece by piece, cutting 2½-inch squares. Sew the squares into A and B segments, as shown, pressing the seams toward the darkest fabric. Join the segments to complete the block.

ADDING THE BORDERS

Step 1. Refer to page 119 in "Quiltmaking Basics" for complete details on adding borders with mitered corners. To determine the correct length to make the side borders, measure the quilt top vertically through the center. To this measurement add two times the finished width of the border (6 inches × 2) plus approximately 5 inches. This is the length you need to make the two side borders. In the same manner, measure the quilt top horizontally through the center, and calculate the length of the top and bottom borders.

Step 2. Sew the 6-inch-wide plaid border strips together end to end to make four long borders, then trim them to the exact length needed. For the twin-size quilt, you'll need two strips each for the top and bottom borders and two and a half strips each for the side borders. The double- and queen-size quilts require two and a half strips for each border.

Step 3. Pin and sew the four borders to the quilt top, matching the midpoint of each border to the midpoint of the side to which it's being added. Refer to "Quiltmaking Basics" on page 119 for complete instructions for adding mitered borders to your quilt. When preparing the miters, be sure to carefully match up the plaid in adjacent borders.

QUILTING AND FINISHING

Step 1. Mark the quilt top for quilting. The quilt shown was quilted with a continuous design of fanlike curves, their arches beginning in the upper left corner and continuing diagonally across and down the quilt.

Step 2. Regardless of which quilt size you've chosen to make, the backing will have to be pieced. To make the most efficient use of the yardage, piece the twin-size back with the seams running vertically and the double- and queen-size backs with the seams running horizontally, as illustrated in **Diagram 6.** To piece the twin-size quilt back, cut the backing fabric crosswise into two equal segments, and trim the selvages.

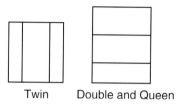

Twin   Double and Queen
Diagram 6

Step 3. Cut one of the segments in half lengthwise, and sew one half to each side of the full-width piece. Press the seams open.

Step 4. To make the backing for the double- and queen-size quilts, cut the backing fabric into three equal segments, and trim the selvages.

Step 5. Sew two of the pieces together along the long side, and press the seam open. Cut a piece approximately 30 inches wide from the third segment. Sew this piece to the joined segment, then press the seam open.

Step 6. Layer the quilt top, batting, and backing, and baste the layers together. Quilt as desired.

Step 7. Make the required length of double-fold binding for your quilt. Refer to page 121 in "Quiltmaking Basics" for complete directions on making and attaching binding. Sew the binding to the quilt using a $\frac{1}{4}$-inch seam allowance.

SUMMER'S END

Color Plan

Photocopy this page and use it to experiment with color schemes for your quilt.

ANTIQUE DOUBLE NINE PATCH
Skill Level: *Easy*

The unusual use of setting squares gives a fresh look to this twin-size 1930s-era Double Nine Patch. Green setting squares and setting triangles around the outer edge create a wide border for the center portion of the quilt, which is set with cream-color squares.

BEFORE YOU BEGIN

The directions for this quilt are written based on using a quick-and-easy method for making Nine-Patch blocks. Strips of fabric are sewn together into strip sets. The strip sets are then cut apart and resewn into blocks. Read through the general construction directions in "Nine-Patch Basics," beginning on page 102, for further details on this technique.

Each Double Nine-Patch block in this quilt is composed of five 3-inch Nine-Patch blocks and four 3-inch setting squares. The Double Nine-Patch blocks are set on point, alternating with cream and green setting squares.

CHOOSING FABRICS

This simple two-color quilt is unusual in its use of two different-color setting squares. The cream squares used in the center area of the quilt provide a sense of brightness, while the darker, green setting squares and triangles around the outside edge act like a border.

The quilt could, of course, be made with more than just two colors. You might also want to try experimenting with the placement of the different-color setting squares. For example, you could create additional patterns by using some of the darker setting squares in the center portion of the quilt.

To help develop your own unique color scheme for the quilt, photocopy the **Color Plan** on page 75, and use crayons or colored pencils to experiment with different color arrangements.

Quilt Sizes		
	Twin (shown)	**Queen**
Finished Quilt Size	76½" × 89¼"	89¼" × 102"
Finished Block Size		
Double Nine Patch	9"	9"
Small Nine Patch	3"	3"
Number of Blocks		
Double Nine Patch	30	42
Small Nine Patch	150	210

Materials		
	Twin	**Queen**
Medium green	4 yards	4⅞ yards
Cream	3½ yards	5 yards
Backing	7½ yards	8⅝ yards
Batting	83" × 96"	96" × 108"
Binding	⅝ yard	¾ yard

NOTE: Yardages are based on 44/45-inch-wide fabrics that are at least 42 inches wide after preshrinking.

69

Cutting Chart

Fabric	Used For	Strip Width	Number of Strips	
			Twin	Queen
Medium green	Side setting triangles	14"	2	3
	Setting squares	9½"	6	7
	Corner setting triangles	7¼"	1	1
	Strip sets	1½"	30	40
Cream	Setting squares	9½"	5	8
	Setting squares	3½"	10	14
	Strip sets	1½"	24	32

CUTTING

All measurements include ¼-inch seam allowances. Referring to the Cutting Chart, cut the required number of strips in the width needed. Cut all strips across the fabric width (crosswise grain).

To make the small setting squares for the Double Nine-Patch blocks, cut the 3½-inch-wide cream strips into 3½-inch squares. For the large cream and green setting squares, cut the 9½-inch-wide strips into 9½-inch squares.

The green side setting triangles and corner setting triangles are cut from squares. To make the side setting triangles, cut the 14-inch-wide strips into 14-inch squares. Cut each square diagonally both ways to get four triangles, as shown in **Diagram 1A**. To make the corner setting triangles, cut the 7¼-inch-wide green strips into 7¼-inch squares. Cut each square in half diagonally to get two triangles, as shown in **1B**. Cutting the triangles from squares in this way puts the straight grain of the fabric on the outside edge of the quilt, where it's needed for stability.

Note: Cut and piece one sample block before cutting all the fabric for the quilt.

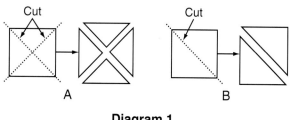

Diagram 1

PIECING THE SMALL NINE-PATCH BLOCKS

The Double Nine-Patch block is made up of five small Nine-Patch blocks and four cream setting squares, as shown in the **Block Diagram.**

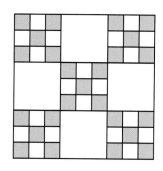

Block Diagram

Each small Nine-Patch block requires two different segment variations, as shown in **Diagram 2.** There are two A segments and one B segment in each block.

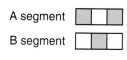

A segment

B segment

Diagram 2

Step 1. The blocks are assembled using a strip-piecing technique. Refer to the Cutting Chart to determine the total number of 1½-inch strips you need to cut from each fabric. Cut all strips across the width of your fabric, from selvage to selvage. The strips should be approximately 42 inches long.

Step 2. To make the A segments, use a ¼-inch seam to sew a green strip to each side of a cream strip, as shown in **Diagram 3**. Press the seam allowances toward the green strips.

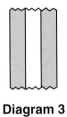

Diagram 3

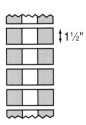

— Sew Easy —

These instructions call for sewing together 42-inch-long strips. If you find that your sewing accuracy diminishes when using these long, narrow strips, cut them in half (approximately 21 inches long each) before sewing them together.

Step 3. Using a rotary cutter and ruler, square up one end of the strip set. Cut 1½-inch-wide segments from the strip set, as shown in **Diagram 4**. You should be able to cut at least 27 segments. Continue making strip sets and cutting them into segments until you have assembled the required number of A segments for your quilt. You need two A segments for each small Nine-Patch block in your quilt.

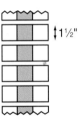

‡1½"

Diagram 4

Step 4. To make the B segments, sew a cream strip to each side of a green strip, as shown in **Diagram 5**. Press both of the seams toward the green strip.

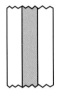

Diagram 5

Step 5. Using a rotary cutter and ruler, square up one end of the strip set. Cut 1½-inch-wide segments from the strip set, as shown in **Diagram 6**. You should be able to cut at least 27 segments. Continue making strip sets and cutting them into segments until you have assembled the required number of B segments for your quilt. You need one B segment for each small Nine-Patch block in your quilt.

‡1½"

Diagram 6

Step 6. Sew two A segments and one B segment together, as shown in **Diagram 7**, matching seams carefully. Since the seam allowances on the segments are pressed in opposite directions, the intersections should fit together tightly. Stitch, using a ¼-inch seam allowance. Press. Repeat until all blocks are assembled.

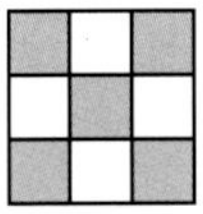

Diagram 7

ASSEMBLING THE DOUBLE NINE-PATCH BLOCKS

Step 1. Lay out five small Nine-Patch blocks and four setting squares into three rows, as shown in **Diagram 8**. Sew the blocks into rows. For less bulk, press the seams toward the setting squares.

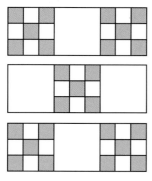

Diagram 8

Step 2. Sew the rows together, matching seams carefully. Press.

Step 3. Repeat until you have assembled the required number of Double Nine-Patch blocks for your quilt.

ASSEMBLING THE QUILT TOP

Step 1. Use a design wall or other flat surface to lay out the Double Nine-Patch blocks, setting squares, side setting triangles, and corner setting triangles. Refer to the appropriate quilt diagram (on this page and page 74) for the correct layout.

Step 2. Referring to the **Assembly Diagram**, sew the blocks and triangles together in diagonal rows, pressing the seams toward the setting squares. Sew the rows together, matching seams carefully. Press.

Twin-Size Quilt Diagram

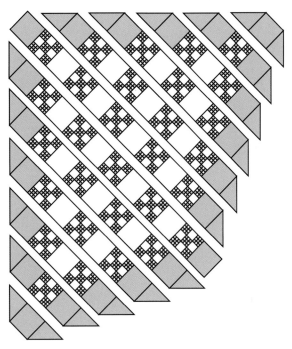

Assembly Diagram

Step 3. Sew the four corner triangles to the quilt top. The triangles are slightly oversize and need to be trimmed after they are added. Use your rotary cutter and ruler to trim the triangles and square up the corners, as shown in **Diagram 9**.

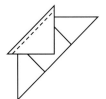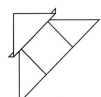

Diagram 9

QUILTING AND FINISHING

Step 1. Mark the quilt top for quilting, if desired. The Double Nine-Patch blocks of the original quilt were stitched with horizontal and vertical lines running through the center of the small squares, as shown in **Diagram 10A**. The same motif was used in the side setting triangles.

The green and cream setting squares were quilted with the motif shown in **10B**.

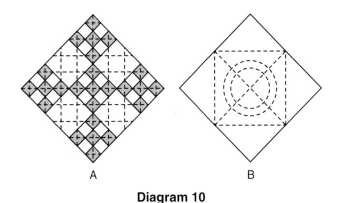

A   B

Diagram 10

Step 2. Regardless of which quilt size you've chosen to make, the backing will have to be pieced. To make the most efficient use of the

Queen-Size Quilt Diagram

yardage, the backs are pieced with the seams running horizontally, as shown in **Diagram 11.**

Diagram 11

Step 3. For either quilt, cut the backing fabric into three equal pieces and trim the selvages. Sew two of the pieces together along the long sides and press the seam open.

Step 4. For the twin-size quilt, cut a piece from the third segment that is 18 inches wide and the

full length of the piece. Sew the piece to the joined segment and press the seam open.

Step 5. For the queen-size quilt, cut a piece from the third segment that is 30 inches wide and the full length of the piece. Sew the piece to the joined segment and press the seam open.

Step 6. Layer the quilt top, batting, and backing, and baste the layers together. Quilt as desired.

Step 7. Referring to the directions on page 121 in "Quiltmaking Basics," make and attach double-fold binding. To calculate the amount of binding needed for the quilt size you are making, add up the length of the four sides of the quilt and add 9 inches. The total is the approximate number of inches of binding you will need.

ANTIQUE DOUBLE NINE PATCH
Color Plan

Photocopy this page and use it to experiment with color schemes for your quilt.

ON THE ROAD AGAIN...
PADUCAH BOUND

Skill Level: *Intermediate*

lever color placement makes this crib-size quilt, with its easy-to-construct blocks, seem more complicated than it actually is. The triangles in the pieced border complete the strong diagonals in the inner quilt. The quilt's unusual title refers to a challenge among a group of the quiltmaker's friends. Each year these friends take their completed challenge projects to the American Quilter's Society show in Paducah, Kentucky, to "show" to each other. The quilt is based on a design by quiltmaker and author Trudie Hughes.

BEFORE YOU BEGIN

Each block in this quilt is composed of a small Nine-Patch block, four corner squares, and four pieced rectangles. In half of the blocks, the small Nine-Patch blocks and corner squares are made with black print fabric, and in the other half they are made with medium gray print fabric. The pieced rectangles, made with magenta print and light gray print, are identical for all the blocks.

The directions are written based on using a quick-and-easy method for making the small Nine-Patch blocks. Strips of fabric are sewn together into strip sets. The strip sets are then cut apart and resewn into blocks. Read through the general construction directions in "Nine-Patch Basics," beginning on page 102, for further details on this technique.

CHOOSING FABRICS

The quiltmaker chose a limited color palette with a high degree

Quilt Sizes

	Crib (shown)	Lap
Finished Quilt Size	36½" × 50½"	50½" × 64½"
Finished Block Size	7"	7"
Number of Blocks		
Black and magenta	12	24
Gray and magenta	12	24

Materials

Fabric	Crib	Lap
Magenta print	1¼ yards	2 yards
Black print	1 yard	1½ yards
Light gray print	1⅜ yards	2 yards
Medium gray print	⅝ yard	⅞ yard
Backing	1⅝ yards	4¼ yards
Batting	42" × 56"	56" × 70"
Binding	⅜ yard	½ yard

NOTE: Yardages are based on 44/45-inch-wide fabrics that are at least 42 inches wide after preshrinking.

of contrast, creating a bold, graphic image. To add movement and energy, she used fabrics with interesting visual textures. For example, the magenta fabric used in the original quilt is a print, but it "reads" as a solid. In other words, it gives the overall appearance of a solid color but has a texture of dark lines, which break

Cutting Chart

Fabric	Used For	Strip Width	Number of Strips	
			Crib	Lap
Magenta print	Inner border triangles	5⅜"	1	1
	Template B	2⅞"	7	14
	Strip sets	1½"	6	8
Black print	Outer border	2¾"	5	7
	Block corners	2½"	3	6
	Strip sets	1½"	3	5
Light gray print	Template A/A reverse	2½"	9	18
	Inner border triangles	2⅞"	1	1
	Inner border segments	2½"	6	7
Medium gray print	Block corners	2½"	3	6
	Strip sets	1½"	3	5

the monotony and help your eyes move across the quilt top. The texture is more apparent in the medium gray print and light gray print fabrics, where it adds depth and dimension to the design.

You may choose to work with more or fewer fabrics to create a different-looking quilt. For best results, make sure there is strong contrast between at least two of the fabrics—the background (light gray in the quilt shown) and the fabric used to create the diagonal pattern (magenta in the quilt shown).

To help develop your own unique color scheme for the quilt, photocopy the **Color Plan** on page 84, and use crayons or colored pencils to experiment with different color arrangements.

CUTTING

All measurements include ¼-inch seam allowances. Referring to the Cutting Chart, cut the required number of strips in the width needed. Cut all strips across the fabric width (crosswise grain).

Make templates for pieces A and A reverse and

B, using the full-size patterns on page 85. Refer to page 116 in "Quiltmaking Basics" for complete details on making and using templates. For the A and A reverse pieces, cut 2½-inch-wide strips from the light gray fabric. Use the template right side up to cut the A pieces from the strips. Turn the template over and cut the A reverse pieces from the strips. You will need two A and two A reverse pieces for each block in your quilt. In the same manner, cut the magenta fabric into 2⅞-inch-wide strips. Use template B to cut four B pieces for each block in your quilt.

The block corners are cut from 2½-inch-wide strips. Cut the black and medium gray 2½-inch strips into 2½-inch squares. You will need four squares for each block.

You will need two sizes of triangles to make the pieced inner border. For the magenta triangles, cut the 5⅜-inch magenta strip into 5⅜-inch squares. You will need three squares for the crib quilt and four squares for the lap-size quilt. Cut each square in half diagonally both ways, as shown in **Diagram 1A**, producing four triangles from each square. For the light gray triangles, cut the 2⅞-inch strip into 2⅞-inch squares. Cut each square in half diagonally, as shown in **1B**.

Note: Cut and piece one sample block before cutting all the fabric for the quilt.

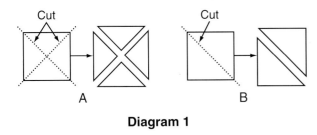

Diagram 1

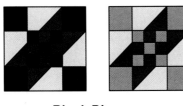

— Sew Easy

Pieces traced with a template are often slightly larger than their rotary-cut counterparts due to the extra width added by drawing lines around the initial template image. Minimize distortion by using a fine-line marker or sharp pencil, then cut the fabric pieces along the inner portion of the marked line rather than along its outer edge.

PIECING THE BLOCKS

Each block in the quilt contains a small Nine-Patch block, four corner squares, and four pieced rectangles. The blocks are made in two different color schemes—black and magenta, and medium gray and magenta—as shown in the **Block Diagram**. Except for the color, the blocks are identical.

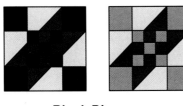

Block Diagram

Making the Small Nine-Patch Blocks

You will need small Nine-Patch blocks in two different color variations, as shown in **Diagram 2**. For illustration purposes, only the black-and-magenta blocks are shown in the diagrams that follow. Repeat all steps to make the required number of medium gray-and-magenta small Nine-Patch blocks.

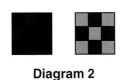

Diagram 2

The blocks are assembled using a strip-piecing technique. Each small Nine-Patch block requires two different segment variations, as shown in **Diagram 3**.

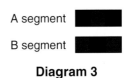

A segment

B segment

Diagram 3

Step 1. Refer to the Cutting Chart to determine the total number of 1½-inch strips you need to cut from each fabric. Cut all strips across the width of your fabric, from selvage to selvage. The strips should be approximately 42 inches long.

Step 2. To make the A segments for the black-and-magenta blocks, use a ¼-inch seam to sew a black strip to each side of a magenta strip, as shown in **Diagram 4A**. Press the seam allowances toward the black strips.

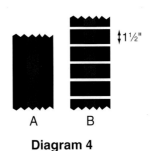

A   B

Diagram 4

Step 3. Using a rotary cutter and ruler, square up one end of the strip set. Cut 1½-inch-wide segments from the strip set, as shown in **4B** on page 79. You should be able to cut at least 27 segments. Continue making strip sets and cutting them into segments until you have assembled the required number of black-and-magenta A segments for your quilt. You need two A segments for each small Nine-Patch block in your quilt. Repeat to make the medium gray-and-magenta A segments.

Step 4. To make the B segments for the black-and-magenta blocks, sew a magenta strip to each side of a black strip, as shown in **Diagram 5A**. Press the seams toward the black strip.

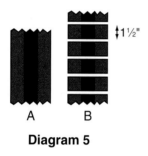

Diagram 5

Step 5. Using a rotary cutter and ruler, square up one end of the strip set. Cut 1½-inch-wide segments from the strip set, as shown in **5B**. You should be able to cut at least 27 segments. Continue making strip sets and cutting them into segments until you have assembled the required number of B segments for your quilt. You need one B segment for each small Nine-Patch block in your quilt. Repeat to make the medium gray-and-magenta B segments.

Step 6. Sew two A segments and one B segment together, as shown in **Diagram 6**, matching seams carefully. Since the seam allowances on the segments are pressed in opposite directions, the intersections should fit together tightly. Stitch, using a ¼-inch seam allowance. Press. Complete all the black-and-magenta blocks, then repeat for the medium gray-and-magenta blocks.

Diagram 6

Making the Pieced Rectangles

Step 1. Each block has four pieced rectangles: two made from a light gray A piece and a magenta B piece and two made from a light gray A reverse piece and a magenta B piece. Place a light gray A piece right sides together with a magenta B piece and align the edges. Using a ¼-inch seam allowance, stitch the pieces together, as shown in **Diagram 7A**. Open up the pieces and carefully press the seam allowance toward the magenta piece. See **7B**. Repeat, pairing each remaining light gray A piece with a magenta B piece.

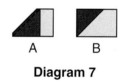

Diagram 7

Step 2. In the same manner, stitch each light gray A reverse piece to a magenta B piece. Open up the pieces and carefully press the seam allowances toward the magenta fabric. The resulting segments will be a mirror image of the Step 1 segments.

ASSEMBLING THE BLOCKS

Step 1. To complete the black-and-magenta blocks, begin by sewing a 2½-inch black block corner to each side of an AB unit, as shown in **Diagram 8**. Press the seams toward the AB unit. Repeat, making a second identical unit.

Diagram 8

Step 2. Sew a reverse AB unit to each side of a black-and-magenta small Nine-Patch block, as shown in **Diagram 9**. Press the seams away from the Nine-Patch block.

Diagram 9

Step 3. As shown in **Diagram 10**, sew a Step 1 section to the top and bottom of the Step 2 section, making sure they are positioned correctly. Repeat, making the total number of black-and-magenta blocks required for your quilt size.

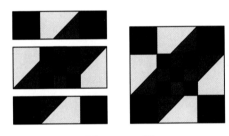

Diagram 10

Step 4. In the same manner, assemble the gray-and-magenta blocks, using the medium gray-and-magenta small Nine-Patch blocks and the medium gray corner squares.

ASSEMBLING THE QUILT TOP

Step 1. Use a design wall or other flat surface to lay out the blocks. Alternate the black-and-magenta blocks with the medium gray-and-magenta blocks, referring to the appropriate quilt diagram for correct layout for your quilt.

Step 2. Sew the blocks together in rows, pressing the seams in opposite directions from row to row. Sew the rows together, pressing seams carefully.

Crib-Size Quilt Diagram

MAKING THE PIECED INNER BORDER

The pieced border is made from light gray fabric combined with magenta triangles to complete the strong diagonal lines of the quilt design. You will piece the inner border first, then join the inner border to the outer border, and then add them to the quilt top as a unit.

Step 1. Sew a light gray triangle to the two shorter sides of each magenta triangle, as shown in **Diagram 11**. These units will be combined with segments of 2½-inch-wide light gray fabric to complete the border.

Diagram 11

Lap-Size Quilt Diagram

Step 2. Refer to the appropriate quilt diagram to understand how the border relates to the quilt top. There are 10-inch-long (finished length) segments of light gray fabric between each of the triangle units made in Step 1. For the crib quilt, cut two 10½-inch-long segments for each side border and one segment each for the top and bottom borders. For the lap-size quilt, cut three 10½-inch-long segments for each side border and two each for the top and bottom borders.

The border corners are mitered. To complete the border strip and allow enough extra to miter the corners for either quilt, cut eight 18-inch-long segments—one for each end of each border strip.

Step 3. Join the Step 1 triangle units with the 10½-inch light gray segments, as shown in **Diagram 12.** Make sure the tips of the triangles are all pointing in the same direction. For the crib quilt, you will have three triangle units and two segments for each side border and two triangle units and one segment each for the top and bottom borders. For the lap-size quilt, you will have four triangle units and three segments for

Diagram 12

each side border and three triangle units and two segments each for the top and bottom borders. Add the 18-inch-long segments to each end of each border strip.

Step 4. Compare each completed border strip to the assembled quilt top. The magenta triangle points in the border should line up with the corresponding magenta B pieces in the blocks, ensuring a smooth line of color from the inner quilt out into the border. Some fullness can be eased in when the border is sewn, but if there is too much excess to ease in, it may be necessary to make slight adjustments in one or more seams joining the border units.

Adding the Borders

Step 1. The pieced inner border will be joined to the outer border, then the two will be sewn to the quilt top as a unit. You will need four outer border strips that are the same length as the corresponding pieced inner border strips. Sew the 2¾-inch-wide black border strips together end to end to make long borders, then trim them to the exact length needed. For the crib quilt, you'll need one and a half strips each for the side borders. The top and bottom borders will need just a few extra inches, not a full half-strip. Measure against the pieced border to determine how much you need, but don't cut a full strip for this little bit of extra; you should be able to piece it from scraps. For the lap-size quilt, you'll need two strips each for the side borders and one and a half strips each for the top and bottom borders.

Step 2. Sew the pieced inner borders and the outer borders together, making four border sets. Make sure you sew the outer border to the correct edge of the inner border so that the triangle points will be facing in the right direction when the borders are added to the quilt.

Step 3. Pin and sew the four borders to the quilt top, referring to page 119 in "Quiltmaking Basics" for complete instructions on adding mitered borders to your quilt.

Quilting and Finishing

Step 1. Mark the quilt top for quilting, if desired. The quilt shown is free-motion machine quilted.

Step 2. If you are making the crib quilt, the backing does not have to be pieced. **Note:** This assumes that your backing fabric is at least 42 inches wide, as specified in the Materials table on page 77. If your fabric is less than 42 inches wide, it may be necessary to add a narrow piece to one edge of the backing. The backing fabric should be at least 3 inches larger than the quilt top on all four sides.

Step 3. The backing for the lap-size quilt will have to be pieced. To make the most efficient use of the yardage, piece the back so that the seams run horizontally across the quilt, as illustrated in **Diagram 13**. To begin, cut the backing fabric crosswise into two equal pieces, and trim the selvages.

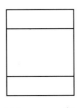

Diagram 13

Step 4. Cut one of the pieces in half lengthwise, and sew one half to each side of the full-width piece. Press the seams open.

Step 5. Layer the quilt top, batting, and backing, and baste the layers together. Quilt as desired.

Step 6. Referring to the directions on page 121 in "Quiltmaking Basics," make and attach double-fold binding. To calculate the amount of binding needed for the quilt size you are making, add up the length of the four sides of the quilt and add 9 inches. The total is the approximate number of inches of binding you will need.

ON THE ROAD AGAIN...
PADUCAH BOUND
Color Plan

Photocopy this page and use it to experiment with color schemes for your quilt.

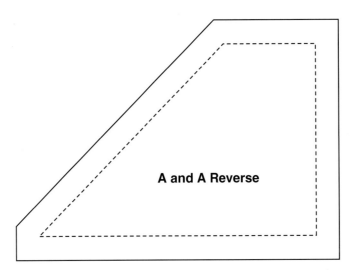

A and A Reverse

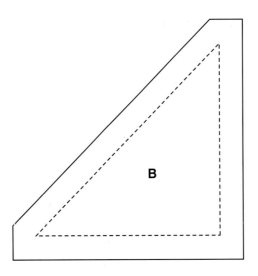

B

MAGIC CROSS NINE PATCH
Skill Level: *Challenging*

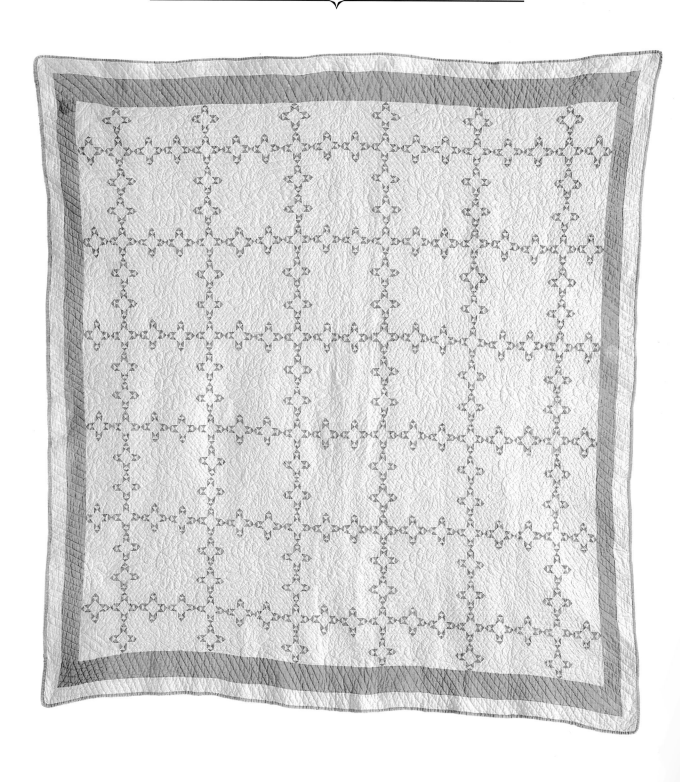

he Nine-Patch blocks in this unusual antique quilt are composed of tiny star blocks. The star blocks appear to be a variation of the pattern identified as the Magic Cross Design in Barbara Brackman's Encyclopedia of Pieced Quilt Patterns. This wonderful lap-size quilt is signed "W. N. Keener, 1878." The present owner obtained the quilt from an estate in Sarcoxie, Missouri; sadly, no further information is known about its long life.

BEFORE YOU BEGIN

Each Nine-Patch block in this quilt is composed of five 2½-inch Magic Cross star blocks. The star blocks are composed of a center square surrounded by 12 triangle squares. The directions are written based on using a grid method to make the ⅝-inch triangle squares. This technique eliminates the need to handle individual tiny triangles, and it makes accurate piecing faster and easier. Read through the general construction directions in "Nine-Patch Basics," beginning on page 102, for further details on this technique.

CHOOSING FABRICS

Keeping the color scheme simple by using just two colors allows the pattern to really take center stage. In this case, the gold stars seem to sparkle against the white background.

The quilt could, of course, be made with more than just two colors. In that case, introducing additional colors into the pattern would result in a quilt with a very different feeling.

To help develop your own unique color scheme for the quilt you are making, photocopy the **Color Plan** on page 93, and use crayons or colored pencils to experiment with different color arrangements.

Quilt Sizes

	Wallhanging	Lap (shown)
Finished Quilt Size	48½" × 51½"	69¾" × 72¾"
Finished Block Size		
Nine Patch	7½"	7½"
Magic Cross	2½"	2½"
Number of Blocks		
Nine Patch	16	36
Magic Cross	80	180

Materials

	Wallhanging	Lap
White	3¼ yards	6½ yards
Gold	1¾ yards	3¼ yards
Backing	3½ yards	4¾ yards
Batting	55" × 58"	76" × 79"
Binding	½ yard	⅝ yard

NOTE: *Yardages are based on 44/45-inch-wide fabrics that are at least 42 inches wide after preshrinking.*

Cutting Chart

Fabric	Used For	Strip Width	Number of Strips Wallhanging	Lap
White	Side setting triangles	11⅞"	1	2
	Setting squares	8"	2	5
	Corner setting triangles	6⅜"	1	1
	Triangle squares	10"	4	9
	Small setting squares	3"	5	11
	Outer border	2"	6	8
	Block centers	1¾"	4	8
Gold	Top and bottom inner border	3½"	3	3
	Side inner border	2"	2	3
	Triangle squares	10"	4	9

CUTTING

All measurements include ¼-inch seam allowances. Referring to the Cutting Chart, cut the required number of strips in the width needed. Cut all strips across the fabric width (crosswise grain).

Cut the 10-inch-wide white and gold strips into 8½ × 10-inch rectangles. These rectangles will be used to make the triangle squares.

To make the small setting squares for the Nine-Patch blocks, cut the 3-inch-wide white strips into 3-inch squares. For the large setting squares, cut the 8-inch-wide white strips into 8-inch squares. For the Magic Cross block centers, cut the 1¾-inch-wide white strips into 1¾-inch squares.

The side setting triangles and corner setting triangles are cut from squares. To make the side setting triangles, cut the 11⅞-inch-wide white strips into 11⅞-inch squares. Cut each square diagonally both ways to get four triangles, as shown in **Diagram 1A.** To make the corner setting triangles, cut the 6⅜-inch-wide white strips into 6⅜-inch squares. Cut each square in half diagonally, as shown in **1B.** Cutting the triangles from squares in this way puts the straight grain of the fabric on the outside edge of the quilt, where it's needed for stability.

Note: Cut and piece one sample block before cutting all the fabric for the quilt.

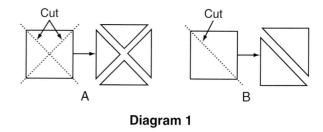

Diagram 1

PIECING THE MAGIC CROSS BLOCKS

Each Nine-Patch block in this quilt contains five 2½-inch Magic Cross blocks and four 2½-inch setting squares, as shown in the **Block Diagram.** Each Magic Cross block contains twelve ⅝-inch triangle squares. The triangle squares are pieced using the grid method.

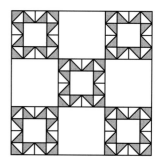

Block Diagram

Step 1. Working on the wrong side of an 8½ × 10-inch rectangle of white fabric, use a pencil or permanent marker to draw a grid of thirty 1½-inch squares, as shown in **Diagram 2A.** Draw the grid so it is at least ½ inch in from the raw edges of the fabric. Referring to **2B,** carefully draw a diagonal line through each square in the grid.

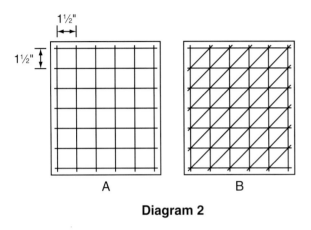

Diagram 2

Step 2. Position the marked white square right sides together with a gold square. Using a ¼-inch seam allowance and a slightly shorter stitch length than normal, stitch along both sides of the diagonal lines, as shown in **Diagram 3.** The shorter stitch length holds the fabrics more securely when you're working with such small pieces. Use the edge of your presser foot as a ¼-inch guide, or draw a line ¼ inch from each side of the diagonal line.

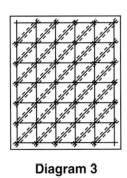

Diagram 3

Step 3. Use a rotary cutter and ruler to cut the grid apart. See page 115 in "Quiltmaking Basics" for complete details on rotary cutting. Cut on all the marked lines, as indicated in **Diagram 4A.**

Carefully press the triangle squares open, pressing the seam toward the gold fabric. Trim off the triangle points at the seam ends, as shown in **4B.** You will get 60 triangle squares from each grid, enough for five Magic Cross blocks (or one Nine-Patch block). Continue marking and cutting triangle squares until you have made the number required for the quilt size you are making.

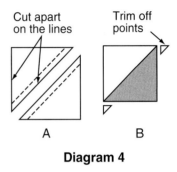

Diagram 4

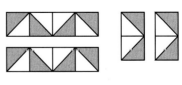

— **Sew Easy**

To make the sewing and cutting lines on the grid easily distinguishable, use different colors of pencils or pens to draw the two types of lines, or devise a marking system that allows you to easily recognize one from another.

Step 4. Referring to **Diagram 5,** lay out 12 triangle squares in four units. Make sure the triangle squares are positioned correctly and stitch them together, as shown, using a ¼-inch seam allowance.

Diagram 5

Step 5. Sew the two shorter units from Step 4 to opposite sides of a 1¾-inch block center, as shown in **Diagram 6**. Press the seams toward the center square.

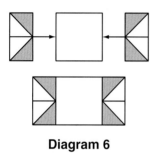

Diagram 6

Note: If seam allowances are too bulky, trim them back as needed or, before assembling star blocks, press open all seams where triangle squares were joined.

Step 6. Sew the two longer units from Step 4 to the top and bottom of the Step 5 section, as shown in **Diagram 7**, matching seams carefully. Repeat until you have assembled the required number of Magic Cross blocks for your quilt.

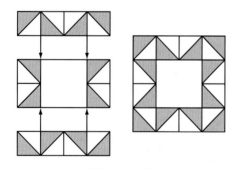

Diagram 7

ASSEMBLING THE NINE-PATCH BLOCKS

Step 1. Sew five Magic Cross blocks and four 3-inch setting squares into three rows, as shown in **Diagram 8**. For flatter seams, press the seam allowances toward the setting squares. **Note:** If you are not pleased with the seam allowances being visible through the white fabric, press the seams toward the Magic Cross blocks. It may be necessary to trim the seams to reduce bulk.

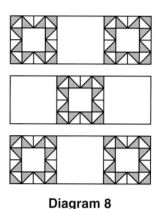

Diagram 8

Sew Easy

Although it is particularly helpful for small sizes, any size triangle square can be assembled using the grid method. Calculate the grid size by adding ⅞ inch to the finished size of your triangle square. For instance, a triangle square with a finished size of 1½ inches would be assembled on a grid made up of 2⅜-inch squares.

Step 2. Sew the rows together, matching seams where blocks meet. Press.

Step 3. Repeat Steps 1 and 2 until you have assembled the required number of Nine-Patch blocks for your quilt.

ASSEMBLING THE QUILT TOP

Step 1. Use a design wall or other flat surface to lay out the Nine-Patch blocks, setting squares, side setting triangles, and corner setting triangles, referring to the **Quilt Diagram** on page 92 for the correct layout. The quilt shown in the diagram is the lap size; the layout for the wallhanging is the same, except it contains four rows of four blocks each.

Step 2. Referring to the **Assembly Diagram**, sew the blocks together in diagonal rows. Press the seams toward the setting squares and side setting triangles. Again, if seam allowances are more visible through the white fabric than desired, press them toward the Nine-Patch blocks. Sew the rows together, matching seams carefully. Press.

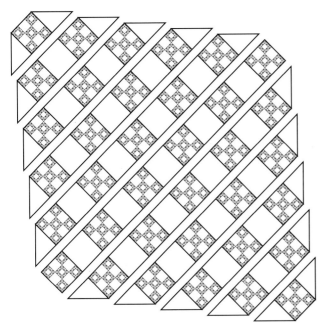

Assembly Diagram

Step 3. Add the four corner setting triangles. The triangles are slightly oversize and need to be trimmed after they are added. Use your rotary cutter and ruler to trim the triangles and square up the corners, as shown in **Diagram 9.** Be sure to trim ¼-inch beyond the edge of the blocks, leaving the seam allowance intact.

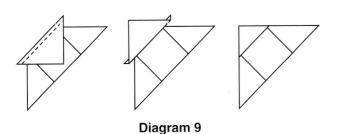

Diagram 9

ADDING THE BORDERS

Step 1. Add the side inner borders first. For the lap-size quilt, begin by cutting one of the 2-inch-wide gold strips in half crosswise and sewing one half each to the two remaining 2-inch-wide strips. The border strips for the wallhanging do not require this extra length.

Step 2. Measure the length of the quilt top, taking the measurement through the vertical center of the quilt rather than along the sides. Trim the side border strips to this length. Fold one of the strips in half crosswise and crease. Unfold it and position it right side down along one side of the quilt, with the crease at the horizontal midpoint. Pin at the midpoint and ends first, then along the length of the entire side, easing in fullness if necessary. Sew the border to the quilt top using a ¼-inch seam allowance. Repeat on the opposite side of the quilt.

Step 3. The top and bottom inner borders must also be lengthened. For the wallhanging, only a few extra inches need to be added to each border. Cut two pieces approximately 6 inches long from one 3½-inch gold strip, and sew one piece each to the two remaining 3½-inch gold strips. For the lap-size quilt, cut one 3½-inch gold strip in half crosswise, and sew one half each to the two remaining 3½-inch gold strips. Measure the width of the quilt, taking the measurement through the horizontal center of the quilt and including the side borders. Trim the strips to this exact length.

Step 4. Fold one strip in half crosswise and crease. Unfold it and position it right side down along the top edge of the quilt, matching the crease to the vertical midpoint. Pin at the midpoint and ends first, then across the entire width of the quilt, easing in fullness if necessary. Stitch, using a ¼-inch seam allowance. Repeat on the bottom edge of the quilt.

Step 5. In the same manner, prepare and add the outer borders to the quilt, adding the side borders first, then the top and bottom. For the lap-size quilt, sew the strips together in pairs to make

Quilt Diagram

four long borders. For the wallhanging, join one and a half strips for each of the four borders. Measure, trim the strips to length, and add them to the quilt.

QUILTING AND FINISHING

Step 1. Mark the quilt top for quilting. The quilt shown is heavily quilted, with a circular feather pattern in the setting squares and side setting triangles and diagonal lines in the borders.

Step 2. Regardless of which quilt size you've chosen to make, the backing will have to be pieced. Cut the backing fabric crosswise into two equal pieces, and trim the selvages.

Step 3. Cut one of the pieces in half lengthwise, and sew one half to each side of the full-width piece, as shown in **Diagram 10**. Press the seams open.

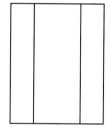

Diagram 10

Step 4. Layer the quilt top, batting, and backing, and baste the layers together. Quilt as desired.

Step 5. Referring to the directions on page 121 in "Quiltmaking Basics," make and attach double-fold binding. To calculate the amount of binding needed for the quilt size you are making, add up the length of the four sides of the quilt and add 9 inches. The total is the approximate number of inches of binding you will need.

MAGIC CROSS NINE PATCH

Color Plan

Photocopy this page and use it to experiment with color schemes for your quilt.
To maximize the space for coloring, only the upper left corner of the quilt is shown.
Make four photocopies and tape them together to complete the quilt.

PERKIOMEN VALLEY SPLIT NINE PATCH

Skill Level: *Intermediate*

his quilt is a beautiful example of a traditional design found in and around the Perkiomen Valley in Montgomery County, Pennsylvania. The setting of the blocks is intended to represent the hills and valleys of the region. Although the origin of the design is unknown, earliest examples date from the early part of this century. Little is known about this particular quilt, although its fabrics would seem to place it in the 1920s. At the time it was made, its size would have made it suitable as a topper for a bed. By today's standards, however, it's more appropriate as a large lap-size quilt or a very large wallhanging.

BEFORE YOU BEGIN

This quilt is composed of Nine-Patch blocks split diagonally into dark and light halves. The directions are written based on using an easy strip-piecing technique for making the Split Nine-Patch blocks. Strips of fabric are sewn together into strip sets. The strip sets are then cut apart and resewn into half-blocks, which are trimmed to the exact size with the help of a triangle template. Read through the general construction directions in "Nine-Patch Basics," beginning on page 102, for further details on strip piecing.

It might also be helpful to read through the instructions a few times before beginning to be sure you understand the technique.

CHOOSING FABRICS

The fabrics in the quilt shown are an interesting combination of bold reds and blues with soft pastels and floral prints. Generous splashes of yellow and a bubble-gum pink border add to the energy of this dynamic quilt.

Choose fabrics in four values: dark, medium dark, light, and medium light. For best results, try to select fabrics that vary in print and scale as well as in value and color. For example, include large- and small-scale prints in both geometrics and florals.

Quilt Size	
Finished Quilt Size	75½" × 75½"
Finished Block Size	6¾"
Number of Blocks	100

Because specific value placement is critical to the overall design of this quilt, no variations in size or layout are provided.

Materials	
Fabric	**Amount**
Assorted darks	3 yards
Assorted medium darks	1⅜ yards
Assorted lights	3 yards
Assorted medium lights	1⅜ yards
Pink	1¼ yards
Backing	5 yards
Batting	82" × 82"
Binding	⅝ yard

NOTE: *Yardages are based on 44/45-inch-wide fabrics that are at least 42 inches wide after preshrinking.*

Cutting Chart

Fabric	Used For	Strip Width	Number of Strips
Assorted darks	Strip sets	2¾"	8
	Strip sets	3¼"	23
Assorted medium darks	Strip sets	2¾"	15
Assorted lights	Strip sets	2¾"	8
	Strip sets	3¼"	23
Assorted medium lights	Strip sets	2¾"	15
Pink	Border	4½"	8

To help develop your own unique color scheme for the quilt, photocopy the **Color Plan** on page 101, and use crayons or colored pencils to experiment with different color arrangements.

The yardages shown are generous estimates of the total yardage actually used in the quilt. For best results, use small amounts of many fabrics.

CUTTING

All measurements include ¼-inch seam allowances. Referring to the Cutting Chart, cut the required number of strips in the width needed. Cut all strips across the fabric width.

Make a template to use in trimming the half-blocks. From template plastic or cardboard, cut a 7⅝-inch square, then cut the square in half diagonally to get a triangle template.

Note: Cut and piece one sample block before cutting all the fabric for the quilt.

PIECING THE BLOCKS

Each Split Nine-Patch block contains six different fabrics: two darks and one medium dark for the dark half and two lights and one medium light for the light half. The dark and light halves are assembled separately, then sewn together to produce the block, as illustrated in the **Block Diagram.**

Each half-block contains three units: one segment cut from two different strip sets, plus a triangle. You will make the strip sets and cut them into segments, then assemble the segments into half-blocks. Each pair of strip sets will result in seven half-blocks. For illustration purposes, only the dark half is shown in the diagrams that follow. The procedure for piecing the light half of the block is exactly the same.

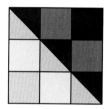

Block Diagram

Step 1. Select one medium dark fabric and two different dark fabrics for the first pair of strip sets. You will need one 2¾-inch-wide medium dark strip, one 2¾-inch-wide dark strip, and two matching 3¼-inch-wide dark strips. Cut the long strips in half so that you are working with strips that are approximately 21 inches long. From one of the 3¼-inch-wide dark strips, cut four 3¼-inch squares.

Step 2. To make the first strip set, sew a 3¼-inch dark strip to a 2¾-inch medium dark strip, as shown in **Diagram 1.** Sew the 2¾-inch dark strip to the opposite side of the medium dark strip. Press the seams toward the dark strips.

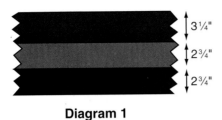

Diagram 1

Diagram 4

Step 3. Use a rotary cutter and ruler to square up one end of the strip set. See page 115 in "Quiltmaking Basics" for complete details on rotary cutting. Cut seven 2¾-inch segments from the strip set, as shown in **Diagram 2.** If your fabric was more than 42 inches wide to begin with, you may be able to cut eight segments. Set the segments aside, stacking them with like fabrics on top of each other.

Step 6. Cut each of the four 3¼-inch dark squares in half diagonally, as shown in **Diagram 5,** producing eight triangles. Stack these triangles near the other cut segments.

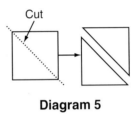

Diagram 5

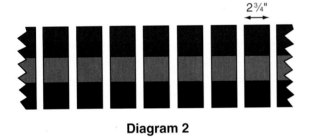

Diagram 2

Step 7. You now have three stacks: two stacks of strip-pieced segments and one stack of triangles. Sew one segment from each stack together, as shown in **Diagram 6,** matching seams carefully. Press the seams toward the dark triangle. Repeat with the remaining segments, making a total of seven identical half-blocks.

Step 4. To make the second strip set, sew a 3¼-inch dark strip to one side of the remaining 2¾-inch medium dark strip, as shown in **Diagram 3.** Press the seam toward the medium dark strip. You will have one 3¼ × 21-inch and one 2¾ × 21-inch dark strip left for another strip set.

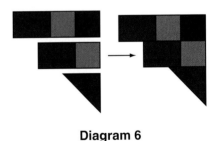

Diagram 6

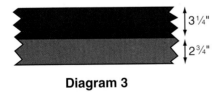

Diagram 3

········ Sew Quick ········

A gridded pressing aid will help you make sure the block corners are square. These handy devices are available as covers for your entire ironing board or as small, portable marked pads.

Step 5. Using a rotary cutter and ruler, square up one end of the strip set, then cut seven 2¾-inch segments from it, as shown in **Diagram 4.** Set the segments aside, stacking them with like fabrics on top of each other.

Step 8. Before they can be used, the half-blocks must be trimmed to the correct size. Align the two short sides of the triangle template to the corresponding sides of a half-block, as shown in **Diagram 7.** Holding the template and fabric firmly in place with a plastic ruler, trim along the long diagonal side of the template, making the block exactly the same size as the template. Repeat with the remaining half-blocks. They are now ready for use.

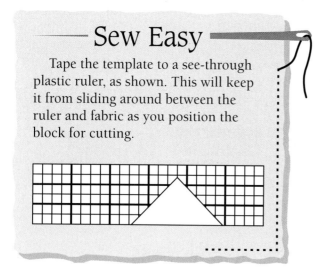

Diagram 7

=== Sew Easy ===

Tape the template to a see-through plastic ruler, as shown. This will keep it from sliding around between the ruler and fabric as you position the block for cutting.

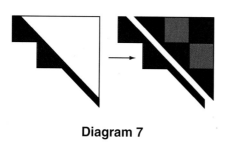

=== Sew Easy ===

If you desire a scrappier quilt, use shorter pieces of fabric to assemble the strip sets. Using strips that are 11½ inches long will produce four segments per strip set, resulting in four half-blocks of the same fabric combination instead of eight. You will need a total of 25 of each strip set combination if you use the shorter length.

two different 3¼-inch light strips, and one 2¾-inch medium light strip. Assemble the fabric into strip sets and construct the half-blocks in the same manner as for the dark half-blocks. The two strip sets for the light half-blocks would look like the ones shown in **Diagram 8.**

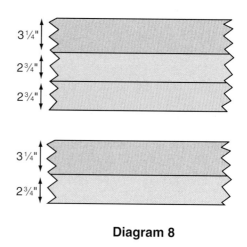

Diagram 8

Step 9. Choose 14 additional sets of fabric, cutting and sewing pieces for each set exactly as you did with the first set. If your fabric is slightly wider and you are able to cut eight segments from each set, you will need fewer total strip sets. Make a total of 100 dark half-blocks.

Step 10. To make the light half-blocks, repeat Steps 2 through 9, using one 2¾-inch light strip,

ASSEMBLING THE NINE-PATCH BLOCKS

Step 1. Align a dark half-block and a light half-block with right sides together. Carefully match seams where the triangles meet along the diagonal edge, pinning if necessary to hold the block halves in place. Using a standard ¼-inch seam allow-

ance, sew half-blocks together, as shown in
Diagram 9. Press the seam allowance to one side.

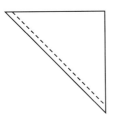

Diagram 9

Step 2. Repeat, assembling a total of 100 Split
Nine-Patch blocks. For best results, avoid sewing
an entire batch of like light halves to another
batch of like dark halves.

Spray a bit of starch or sizing on the
back side of the block to help keep the diagonal seam in place during pressing.

ASSEMBLING THE QUILT TOP

Step 1. Use a design wall or flat surface to
arrange the blocks, as shown in the **Quilt
Diagram.** Pay close attention to the placement of
the blocks.

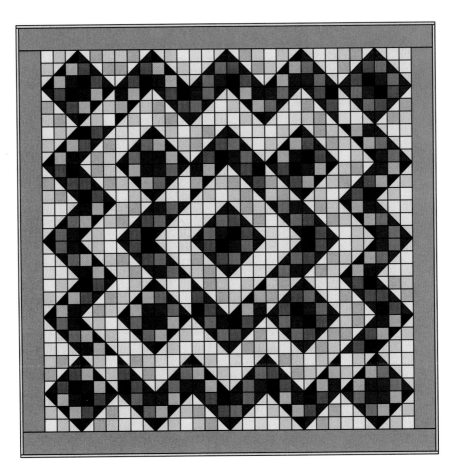

Quilt Diagram

Step 2. Sew the blocks into rows, as shown in the **Assembly Diagram.** Press the seams in opposite directions from row to row.

Assembly Diagram

Step 3. Sew the rows together, matching seams where blocks meet. Since the seam allowances are pressed in opposite directions, the intersections should fit together tightly. Press the quilt top.

Adding the Borders

Step 1. Begin by sewing the 4½-inch-wide border strips together in pairs, making four long border strips. Measure the width of the quilt top, taking the measurement through the horizontal center of the quilt rather than along the edge. Trim two of the border strips to this exact length.

Step 2. Fold one strip in half crosswise and crease. Unfold it and position it right side down along the top edge of the quilt, with the crease at the vertical midpoint. Pin at the midpoint and ends first, then along the length of the entire edge, easing in fullness if necessary. Sew the border to the quilt using a ¼-inch seam allowance. Press the seam allowance toward the border. Repeat on the bottom edge of the quilt.

Step 3. Measure the length of the quilt, taking the measurement through the vertical center of the quilt and including the top and bottom borders. Trim the two remaining border strips to this exact length.

Step 4. Fold one strip in half crosswise and crease. Unfold it and position it right side down along one side of the quilt, matching the crease to the horizontal midpoint. Pin at the midpoint and ends first, then along the entire length of the side, easing in fullness if necessary. Stitch, using a ¼-inch seam allowance. Press the seam allowance toward the border. Repeat on the opposite side of the quilt top.

Quilting and Finishing

Step 1. Mark the quilt top for quilting. The quilt shown is quilted with an X through the center of each square. There are parallel zigzag lines of quilting in the border.

Step 2. To piece the backing, cut the backing fabric crosswise into two equal pieces, and trim the selvages. Cut one of the pieces in half lengthwise, and sew one half to each side of the full-width piece, as shown in **Diagram 10.** Press the seams open.

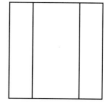

Diagram 10

Step 3. Layer the quilt top, batting, and backing, and baste the layers together. Quilt as desired.

Step 4. Referring to page 121 in "Quiltmaking Basics," make and attach double-fold binding. You will need approximately 313 inches of binding.

PERKIOMEN VALLEY
SPLIT NINE PATCH
Color Plan

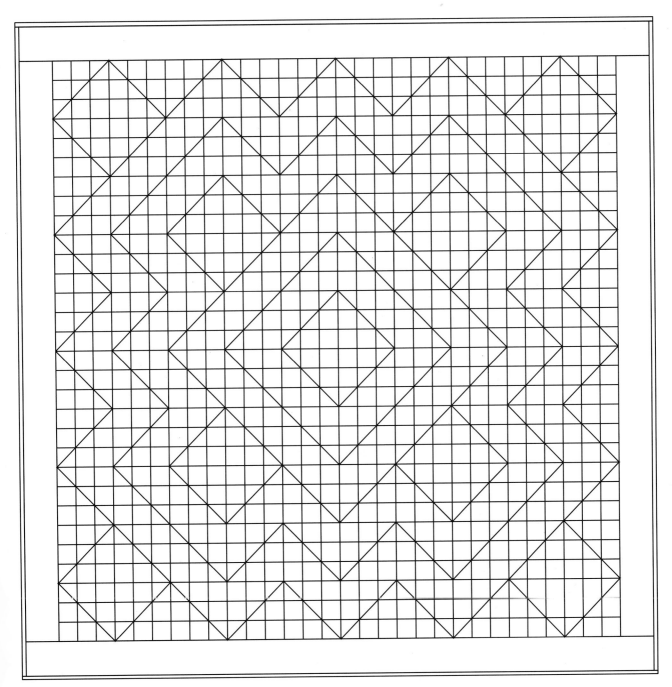

Photocopy this page and use it to experiment with color schemes for your quilt.

NINE-PATCH
BASICS

The step-by-step directions for many of the projects in this book are based on strip-piecing techniques. In this section, you'll find details on this technique as well as helpful information pertaining to Nine-Patch quilts in general. It's a good idea to read through this section before beginning any of the projects in this book.

THE BASIC BLOCK

A Nine Patch, as we use the term here, is any block that can be divided into nine equal units. In its most basic form, the block consists of nine plain squares of fabric. The squares can be set in an alternating dark and light pattern, as shown in **Diagram 1,** or in a more random pattern using a greater range of values. Most often, the block consists of two identical rows (the top and bottom) and one row that differs (in the middle).

Various effects can be created by changing the colors and values used in the blocks. For example, the two variations shown in **Diagram 1** are the same, but they look very different due to the reversed placement of color value. The placement of light and dark fabrics is an important aspect of many Nine-Patch quilts, since it defines the overall pattern by creating a visual link between blocks. These two examples are by no means the only variations possible—value placement is entirely up to you and dependent on the look you want to achieve with your quilt. An example of another option is the Snowball and Nine Patch on page 26. There, the placement of lights and darks is totally random.

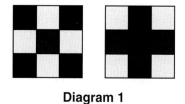

Diagram 1

Beyond changing the color and value placement, you can further vary the Nine-Patch block by dividing the nine individual squares into any number of pieces in any orientation. The Double Nine Patch on page 10 and the Magic Cross Nine Patch on page 86 are both examples of Nine-Patch blocks with divided units. Each block of the Double Nine Patch contains five small, simple Nine-Patch blocks and four plain squares. In the Magic Cross Nine Patch, the quiltmaker chose to place five small stars within the larger Nine-Patch block. Both blocks are illustrated in **Diagram 2.**

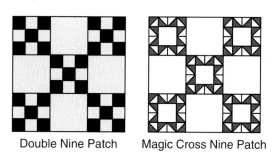

Double Nine Patch   Magic Cross Nine Patch

Diagram 2

ASSEMBLING NINE-PATCH BLOCKS

There are basically two ways to piece Nine-Patch blocks: the traditional method and the strip-piecing method. Unless you intend to make a charm quilt, where no fabric is repeated, most Nine-Patch blocks can be assembled using strip-piecing methods.

With the traditional method, nine squares of fabric are cut and sewn together in three rows of three squares each. If you multiply the time spent cutting, sewing, and pressing for just one block by the number of blocks required for your quilt, the task of piecing traditionally can seem monumental.

With the strip-piecing method, long strips of fabric are sewn together into one large strip set. The seams are pressed, then the strip set is cut apart into short segments, with each segment equal to a row in the block. Three segments are then joined to complete the block. This system eliminates all of the individual cutting, sewing, and pressing steps, allowing you to finish blocks and begin assembling your quilt top in a much shorter time.

Strip-Piecing Basics

Step 1. The first step in strip-piecing is accurately cutting the strips that will be sewn together to make the strip sets. To determine the correct width to cut the strips, first determine the finished size of each square in the Nine-Patch block. (For all of the projects in this book, the correct strip width is provided for you.)

For this example, assume that each square in the Nine-Patch block has a finished size of 1½ inches. If you add the standard ¼-inch seam allowance to each side, the result is a cut size of 2 inches square. Therefore, the correct strip width is 2 inches.

Step 2. Next, determine the strip length. The length is dependent on how many identical segments you want to make. If each Nine-Patch block in the quilt was exactly the same, such as the Double Nine Patch shown on page 10, you would use long strips of fabric cut selvage to selvage so that a large number of identical segments could be assembled and cut at one time. For a scrappy quilt, you would probably want fewer segments of each fabric combination, so shorter strips would be used.

Multiply the finished length of each segment (2 inches) by the number of identical segments you decide to make. For this example, assume you want ten segments, enough for five blocks.

2 inches × 10 segments = 20 inches

Add ½ inch to the total length to allow a bit of extra fabric for squaring up the unit after it is stitched, for a total of 20½ inches.

Step 3. Cut two 2 × 20½-inch strips of dark fabric and one 2 × 20½-inch strip of light fabric. Align a dark strip lengthwise with a light strip, placing right sides together and matching raw edges carefully. Pin in a few places if necessary, then stitch, using a ¼-inch seam. Sew a second dark strip to the opposite side of the light strip to produce the strip set shown in **Diagram 3**.

Diagram 3

> ### Sew Easy
> Each time you add a strip to a strip set, begin sewing at the end opposite from where the seam of the previous strip began. This consistent flip-flopping will help eliminate the warping that often occurs when long strips are sewn together.

Step 4. To press the strip set, place it right side up on the ironing board. Work on one seam at a time. First set the seam by pressing it flat, just as it was sewn. Then open out one of the dark strips and gently glide the side of the iron across the seam. You will be simultaneously pressing the strip flat and pressing the seam allowance toward the dark strip. If necessary, use your fingers to reach under the strip set to guide the seam allowance toward the dark strip. Repeat for the remaining seam allowance.

Press gently. Avoid vigorous back-and-forth motions that might stretch the fabric out of shape.

> ### Sew Easy
> If you have problems sewing an accurate ¼-inch seam on long strips, try working with shorter strips until you are more accustomed to strip piecing.

Step 5. No matter how carefully you align raw edges, the ends of the strip set will probably be slightly uneven. Place a see-through plastic ruler at one end of the strip set, as shown in **Diagram 4.** Be sure to align a horizontal marking on the ruler with one of the seam lines to be sure the cut edge is at a 90 degree angle to the seams.

Cut across the entire width of the strip set with a rotary cutter, slicing away the uneven edge.

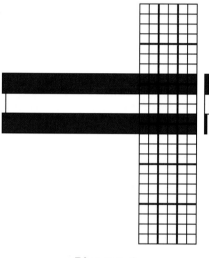

Diagram 4

Step 6. Use your rotary cutter and ruler to cut ten 2-inch-wide segments from the strip, as shown in **Diagram 5.** Be sure to maintain the 90 degree edge by keeping a horizontal line aligned with one of the seams. These ten segments are the top and bottom rows for five Nine-Patch blocks.

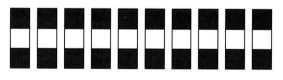

Diagram 5

Step 7. Repeat the construction process to make the segments for the middle row, reversing the light and dark fabric positions, as shown in

Diagram 6. Since this segment is used only once in each block, a shorter strip length will be adequate.

2 inches × 5 segments = 10 inches
Plus ½ inch extra = 10½ inches

Sew the strips together, press the seams toward the dark fabric, then cut the segments. These segments provide the middle row for five Nine-Patch blocks.

Diagram 6

Step 8. To complete one block, sew together two Step 6 segments and one Step 7 segment, matching seams carefully.

MAKING TRIANGLE SQUARES

Several of the quilts in this book contain triangle squares, sometimes called half-square triangles. These are squares that are made up of two equal triangles of different fabrics, as shown in **Diagram 7.**

Diagram 7

There are several ways to construct these squares. One way is to cut two individual triangles, then sew them together along their diagonal edges. With this method, however, the diagonal edge of each triangle is cut along the bias of the fabric, so the fabric will stretch if not handled carefully. A better method—one that avoids working with bias edges—uses a technique that totally eliminates handling individual triangles.

There are two ways of approaching this technique. In the first, you work with individual squares to produce two identical triangle squares. In the second, useful when you need a large number of identical squares, you work on a larger piece of fabric that is marked in a grid. After the fabrics are stitched together, the grid is cut apart into triangle squares.

The Individual Square Method

This method is a good choice if the finished size of your triangle squares is $1\frac{1}{2}$ inches or more or if you want to use a number of different fabrics. For smaller squares or a large number of identical squares, sewing on a grid will often provide faster and more accurate results.

Step 1. To begin, cut one square each from two different fabrics. To determine the correct size to cut the squares, add $\frac{7}{8}$ inch to the finished size of the triangle square. For example, to end up with a 3-inch finished triangle square, cut two squares that are $3\frac{7}{8}$ inches each.

Step 2. Working on the back side of the lighter fabric, use a pencil or fine-point permanent marker to carefully draw a diagonal line from corner to corner, as shown in **Diagram 8A**. Place the square right sides together with the second square and stitch them together, sewing $\frac{1}{4}$ inch from both sides of the diagonal line. See **8B**.

Use the edge of your presser foot as a $\frac{1}{4}$-inch guide, or draw a line $\frac{1}{4}$ inch from each side of the diagonal line. After stitching, cut the square apart on the diagonal line, producing two identical triangle squares.

A technique called chain piecing will help you sew squares at a much faster rate. With this method, sandwiched squares are fed through the sewing machine one after another, without lifting the presser foot or clipping threads on individual segments. The end result is a chain of sewn segments connected to one another by a short length of thread, as shown in **Diagram 9.** Sew one seam of each square, cut the threads apart, then run the squares through the machine again, sewing the second seam.

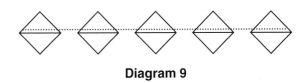

Diagram 9

Sew Easy

To get off to a smooth start, use a folded scrap of fabric as a leader when you begin chain piecing. This keeps the first pair in the chain from bunching up under the presser foot.

The Grid Method

With this method, the fabric is cut oversize, then marked, sewn, and cut apart into individual triangle squares. The technique requires careful marking and sewing. It produces multiples of identical triangle squares and is especially useful when working with very small squares. Like the individual square method, this technique allows you to avoid working with bias edges.

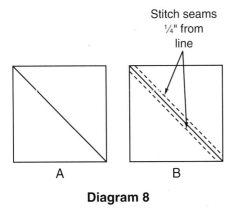

Stitch seams
$\frac{1}{4}$" from
line

A   B

Diagram 8

The grid from the Magic Cross Nine Patch on page 86 is used as an example here.

Step 1. To begin, determine the correct size to cut the fabric. You must know the size of the squares and the number of squares per grid you wish to make. The size of the squares is equal to the finished size of the triangle squares, plus ⅞ inch. Each square in the grid will result in two triangle squares. In this example, the size of the squares is 1½ inches, and the number of squares per grid is 30 (resulting in 60 triangle squares).

A grid of five squares by six squares would require a 7½ × 9-inch piece of fabric. Since it's a good idea to allow a little extra room on each side of the grid, we cut the two pieces of fabric 8½ × 10 inches each.

Step 2. Working on the wrong side of the lighter fabric, use a pencil or permanent marker to draw a grid of squares, as shown in **Diagram 10A.** Draw the grid at least ½ inch in from the raw edges of the fabric. Referring to **10B**, carefully draw a diagonal line through each square in the grid.

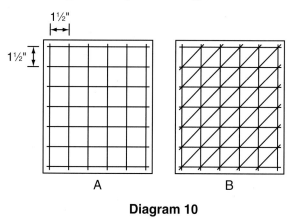

Diagram 10

Step 3. Position the marked fabric right sides together with the second piece of fabric. Using a ¼-inch seam allowance, stitch along both sides of the diagonal lines, as shown in **Diagram 11.** Use the edge of your presser foot as a ¼-inch guide, or draw a line ¼ inch from each side of the diagonal line.

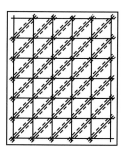

Diagram 11

········· Sew Quick ·········

To save time, don't clip threads at the end of each line of stitches. Simply lift the presser foot, rotate the fabric, insert the needle, and begin the next line of stitching.

Step 4. Use a rotary cutter and ruler to cut the grid apart. Cut on all the marked lines, as indicated in **Diagram 12A.** Carefully press the triangle squares open, pressing the seam toward the darker fabric. Trim off the triangle points at the seam ends, as shown in **12B**. Continue marking and cutting triangle squares until you have the number required for the quilt you are making.

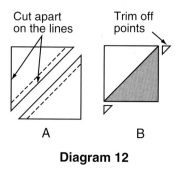

Diagram 12

── Sew Easy ──

To make the sewing and cutting lines on the grid easily distinguishable, use different-color pencils or pens to draw the two types of lines, or devise a marking system that allows you to easily recognize one from another.

QUILT SETTINGS

There are two basic settings for quilt blocks: straight set and diagonal. Both settings are represented in this book.

Straight Sets

In a straight-set quilt, the block sides are parallel to the borders, as shown in **Diagram 13.** Blocks can be set together, set with alternating setting squares, or set with sashing strips.

The top is assembled with blocks sewn together in rows, as shown in **Diagram 14.** In this example, sashing strips separate the individual blocks, creating two types of rows. The rows are then joined together to complete the quilt top.

Diagonal Sets

In a diagonally set quilt, block sides are at a 45 degree angle to the borders. This placement of blocks is called "on point" and is illustrated in **Diagram 15** on page 110.

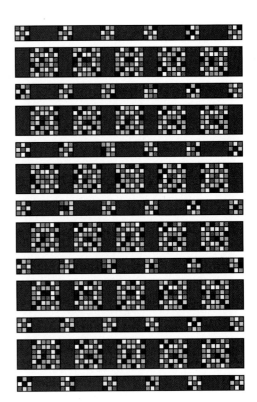

Diagram 14

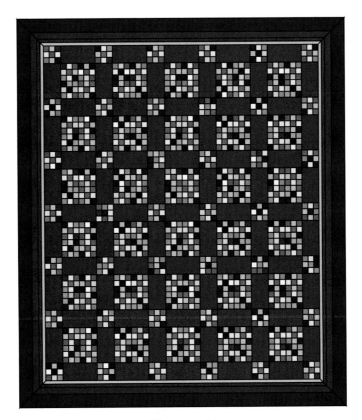

Diagram 13

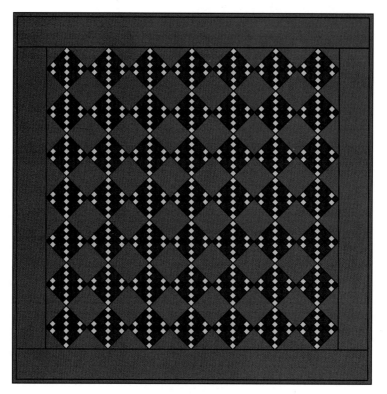

Diagram 15

The blocks can be set together or with alternating setting squares. While these setting squares are sometimes pieced, they are more often plain. The same is true of the side setting triangles and corner setting triangles that are used to fill in the points around the outside edges of the quilt top. Most of the quilts in this book have plain setting squares and triangles; an exception is the Dots and Dashes quilt on page 44.

The blocks in a diagonally set quilt top are first sewn into diagonal rows with triangles at each end, as illustrated in **Diagram 16.** The rows are joined together, then the corner triangles are added.

Setting Squares and Triangles

Setting squares in both straight-set and diagonally set quilts are simply cut the same size as the blocks.

Diagram 16

The side setting triangles and corner setting triangles used in diagonally set quilts must be carefully measured and cut. For best results, cut the triangles from squares, as shown in **Diagram 17**. For the side setting triangles, cut each square diagonally both ways, as shown in **17A**. For the corner setting triangles, cut each square in half diagonally one way, as shown in **17B**. Cutting the triangles from squares in this way puts the straight grain of the fabric on the outside edge of the quilt, where it's needed for stability.

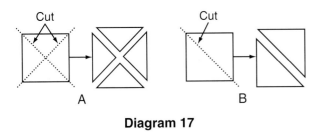

Diagram 17

To measure and cut side setting triangles: Determine the finished diagonal measurement of the quilt block. To do this, multiply the finished length of a block side by 1.41. Round the result up to the nearest $\frac{1}{8}$ inch. Using a 6-inch finished block as an example:

$$6" \times 1.41 = 8.46"$$
$$\text{rounded up to the nearest } \frac{1}{8}" = 8.5" (8\frac{1}{2}")$$

Add $1\frac{1}{4}$ inches to the finished diagonal measurement to determine what size square to cut:

$$8\frac{1}{2}" + 1\frac{1}{4}" = 9\frac{3}{4}"$$

For the side setting triangles on a quilt with 6-inch finished blocks, cut $9\frac{3}{4}$-inch squares. Cut each square diagonally both ways to get four triangles, as shown in **17A**. The resulting triangles will be slightly larger than the size you need; you will trim the excess after sewing the quilt top together.

To measure and cut corner triangles: Determine the finished diagonal measurement of the quilt block. To do this, multiply the finished length of one side of a block by 1.41 and round the result up to the nearest $\frac{1}{8}$ inch. Using the same 6-inch finished block in this example, the finished diagonal measurement is $8\frac{1}{2}$ inches. Divide the finished diagonal measurement by two:

$$8\frac{1}{2}" \div 2 = 4\frac{1}{4}"$$

Add $\frac{7}{8}$ inch to the result:

$$4\frac{1}{4}" + \frac{7}{8}" = 5\frac{1}{8}"$$

For the corner triangles on a quilt that has 6-inch finished blocks, cut $5\frac{1}{8}$-inch squares, then cut the squares in half diagonally one way, as shown in **17B**.

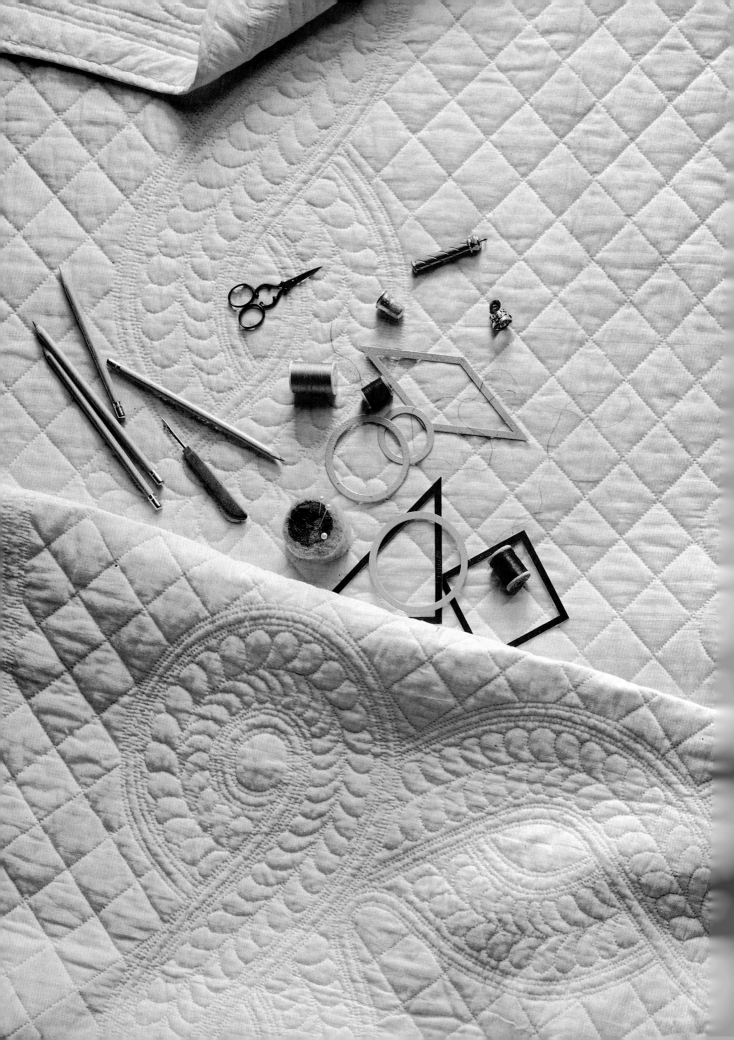

QUILTMAKING
BASICS

This section provides a refresher course in basic quiltmaking techniques. Refer to it as needed; it will help not only with the projects in this book but also with all your quiltmaking.

QUILTMAKER'S BASIC SUPPLY LIST

Here's a list of items you should have on hand before beginning a project.

• **Iron and ironing board:** Make sure these are set up near your sewing machine. Careful pressing leads to accurate piecing.

• **Needles:** The two types of needles commonly used by quilters are *betweens,* short needles used for quilting, and *sharps,* long, very thin needles used for appliqué and hand piecing. The thickness of hand-sewing needles decreases as their size designation increases. For instance, a size 12 needle is smaller than a size 10.

• **Rotary cutter, plastic ruler, and cutting mat:** Fabric can be cut quickly and accurately with rotary-cutting equipment. There are a variety of cutters available, all with slightly different handle styles and safety latches. Rigid, see-through plastic rulers are used with rotary cutters. A 6 × 24-inch ruler is a good size; for the most versatility, be sure it has 45 degree and 60 degree angle markings. A 14-inch square ruler will also be helpful for making sure blocks are square. Always use a special mat with a rotary cutter. The mat protects the work surface and helps to grip the fabric. Purchase the largest mat practical for your sewing area. A good all-purpose size is 18 × 24 inches.

• **Safety pins:** These are generally used to baste quilts for machine quilting. Use rustproof nickel-plated brass safety pins, preferably in size #0.

• **Scissors:** You'll need several pairs of scissors—shears for cutting fabric, general scissors for cutting paper and template plastic, and small, sharp embroidery scissors for trimming threads.

• **Seam ripper:** A seam ripper with a small, extra-fine blade slips easily under any stitch length.

• **Sewing machine:** Any machine with a straight stitch is suitable for piecing quilt blocks. Follow the manufacturer's recommendations for cleaning and servicing your sewing machine.

• **Straight pins:** Choose long, thin pins with glass or plastic heads that are easy to see against fabric so that you don't forget to remove one.

• **Template material:** Sheets of clear and opaque template plastic can be purchased at most quilt or craft shops. Gridded plastic is also available and may help you to draw shapes more easily. Various weights of cardboard can also be used for templates, including common household items like cereal boxes, poster board, and manila file folders.

• **Thimbles:** For hand quilting, a thimble is almost essential. Look for one that fits the finger you use to push the needle. The thimble should be snug enough to stay put when you shake your hand. There should be a bit of space between the end of your finger and the inside of the thimble.

• **Thread:** For hand or machine piecing, 100 percent cotton thread is a traditional favorite. Cotton-covered polyester is also acceptable. For hand quilting, use 100 percent cotton quilting thread. For machine quilting, you may want to try clear nylon thread as the top thread, with cotton thread in the bobbin.

• **Tweezers:** Keep a pair of tweezers handy for removing bits of thread from ripped-out seams and for pulling away scraps of removable foundations. Regular cosmetic tweezers will work fine.

SELECTING AND PREPARING FABRICS

The traditional fabric choice for quilts is 100 percent cotton. It handles well, is easy to care for, presses easily, and frays less than synthetic blends.

The yardages in this book are generous estimates based on 44/45-inch-wide fabrics. It's a good idea to always purchase a bit more fabric than necessary to compensate for shrinkage and occasional cutting errors.

Prewash your fabrics using warm water and a mild soap or detergent. Test for colorfastness by first soaking a scrap in warm water. If colors bleed, set the dye by soaking the whole piece of fabric in a solution of 3 parts cold water to 1 part vinegar. Rinse the fabric several times in warm water. If it still bleeds, don't use it in a quilt that will need laundering—save it for a wallhanging that won't get a lot of use.

After washing, preshrink your fabric by drying it in a dryer on the medium setting. To keep wrinkles under control, remove the fabric from the dryer while it's still slightly damp and press it immediately with a hot iron.

CUTTING FABRIC

The cutting instructions for each project follow the list of materials. Whenever possible, the instructions are written to take advantage of quick rotary-cutting techniques. In addition, some projects include patterns for those who prefer to make templates and scissor cut individual pieces.

Although rotary cutting can be faster and more accurate than scissor cutting, it has one disadvantage: It does not always result in the most efficient use of fabric. In some cases, the method results in long strips of leftover fabric. Don't think of these as waste; just add them to your scrap bag for future projects.

Rotary-Cutting Basics

Follow these two safety rules every time you use a rotary cutter: Always cut *away* from yourself, and always slide the blade guard into place as soon as you stop cutting.

Step 1: You can cut several layers of fabric at a time with a rotary cutter. Fold the fabric with the selvage edges together. You can fold it again if you want, doubling the number of layers to be cut.

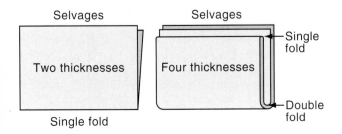

Step 2: To square up the end of the fabric, place a ruled square on the fold and slide a 6 × 24-inch ruler against the side of the square. Hold the ruler in place, remove the square, and cut along the edge of the ruler. If you are left-handed, work from the other end of the fabric.

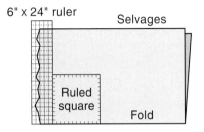

Step 3: For patchwork, cut strips or rectangles on the crosswise grain, then subcut them into smaller pieces as needed. The diagram shows a strip cut into squares.

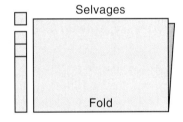

Step 4: A square can be subcut into two triangles by making one diagonal cut (A). Two diagonal cuts yield four squares (B).

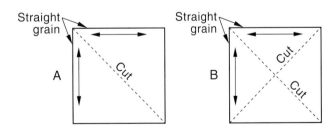

Step 5: Check strips periodically to make sure they're straight and not angled. If they are angled, refold the fabric and square up the edges again.

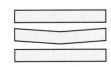

ENLARGING PATTERNS

Every effort has been made to provide full-size pattern pieces. But in some cases, where the pattern piece is too large to fit on the page, the pattern runs at a reduced size. Instructions below the pattern will tell you how much it needs to be enlarged to make it full size. Take the book to a photocopier and enlarge by the percentage indicated on the pattern.

MAKING AND USING TEMPLATES

To make a plastic template, place template plastic over the book page, trace the pattern onto the plastic, and cut out the template. To make a cardboard template, copy the pattern onto tracing paper, glue the paper to the cardboard, and cut out the template. With a permanent marker, record on every template any identification letters and grain lines, as well as the size and name of the block and the number of pieces needed. Always check your templates against the printed pattern for accuracy.

The patchwork patterns in this book are printed with double lines. The inner dashed line is the finished size of the piece, while the outer solid line includes seam allowance.

For hand piecing: Trace the inner line to make finished-size templates. Cut out the templates on the traced line. Draw around the templates on the wrong side of the fabric, leaving ½ inch between pieces. Then mark ¼-inch seam allowances before you cut out the pieces.

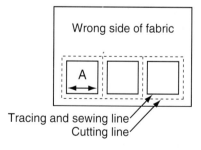

Wrong side of fabric

A

Tracing and sewing line
Cutting line

For machine piecing: Trace the outer solid line on the printed pattern to make templates with seam allowance included. Draw around the templates on the wrong side of the fabric and cut out the pieces on this line.

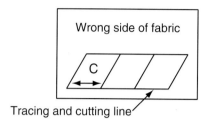

Wrong side of fabric

C

Tracing and cutting line

For appliqué: Appliqué patterns in this book have only a single line and are finished size. Draw around the templates on the right side of the fabric, leaving ½ inch between pieces. Add ⅛- to ¼-inch seam allowances by eye as you cut the pieces.

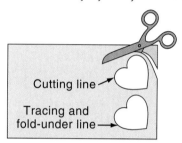

Cutting line

Tracing and
fold-under line

PIECING BASICS

Standard seam allowance for piecing is ¼ inch. Machine sew a sample seam to test the accuracy of the seam allowance; adjust as needed. For hand piecing, the sewing line is marked on the fabric.

Hand Piecing

Cut fabric pieces using finished-size templates. Place the pieces right sides together, match marked seam lines, and pin. Use a running stitch along the marked line, backstitching every four or five stitches and at the beginning and end of the seam.

When you cross seam allowances of previously joined units, leave the seam allowances free. Backstitch just before you cross, slip the needle through the seam allowance, backstitch just after you cross, then resume stitching the seam.

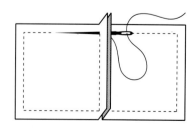

Machine Piecing

Cut the fabric pieces using templates with seam allowances included or using a rotary cutter and ruler without templates. Set the stitch length at 10 to 12 stitches per inch.

Place the fabric pieces right sides together, then sew from raw edge to raw edge. Press seams before crossing them with other seams, pressing toward the darker fabric whenever possible.

Chain piecing: Use this technique when you need to sew more than one of the same type of unit. Place the fabric pieces right sides together and, without lifting the presser foot or cutting the thread, run the pairs through the sewing machine one after another. Once all the units you need have been sewn, snip them apart and press.

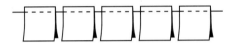

Setting In Pieces

Pattern pieces must sometimes be set into angles created by other pieces, as shown in the diagram. Here, pieces A, B, and C are set into the angles created by the four joined diamond pieces.

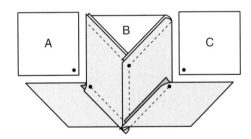

Step 1: Keep the seam allowances open where the piece is to be set in. Begin by sewing the first seam in the usual manner, beginning and ending the seam ¼ inch from the edge of the fabric and backstitching at each end.

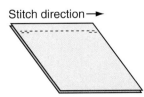

Step 2: Open up the pattern pieces and place the piece to be set in right sides together with one of the first two pieces. Begin the seam ¼ inch from the edge of the fabric and sew to the exact point where the first seam ended, backstitching at the beginning and end of the seam.

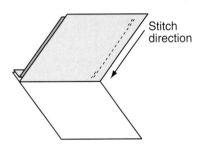

Step 3: Rotate the pattern pieces so that you are ready to sew the final seam. Keeping the seam allowances free, sew from the point where the last seam ended to ¼ inch from the edge of the piece.

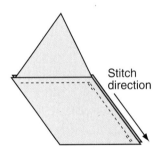

Step 4: Press the seams so that as many of them as possible lie flat. The finished unit should look like the one shown here.

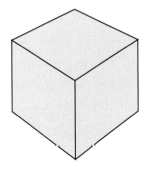

APPLIQUÉ BASICS

Review "Making and Using Templates" to learn how to prepare templates for appliqué. Lightly draw around each template on the right side of the fabric using a pencil or other nonpermanent marker. These are the fold-under lines. Cut out the pieces ⅛ to ¼ inch to the outside of the marked lines.

The Needle-Turn Method

Pin the pieces in position on the background fabric, always working in order from the background to the foreground. For best results, don't turn under or appliqué edges that will be covered by other appliqué pieces. Use a thread color that matches the fabric in the appliqué piece.

Step 1: Bring the needle up from under the appliqué patch exactly on the drawn line. Fold under the seam allowance on the line to neatly encase the knot.

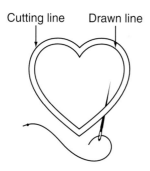

Cutting line   Drawn line

Step 2: Insert the tip of the needle into the background fabric right next to where the thread comes out of the appliqué piece. Bring the needle out of the background fabric approximately ¹⁄₁₆ inch away from and up through the very edge of the fold, completing the first stitch.

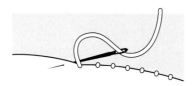

Step 3: Repeat this process for each stitch, using the tip and shank of your appliqué needle to turn under ½-inch-long sections of seam allowance at a time. As you turn under a section, press it flat with your thumb and then stitch it in place, as shown.

PRESSING BASICS

Proper pressing can make a big difference in the appearance of a finished block or quilt top. It allows patchwork to open up to its full size, permits more precise matching of seams, and results in smooth, flat work. Quilters are divided on the issue of whether a steam or dry iron is best; experiment to see which works best for you. Keep these tips in mind:

• Press seam allowances to one side, not open. Whenever possible, press toward the darker fabric. If you find you must press toward a lighter fabric, trim the dark seam allowance slightly to prevent show-through.

• Press seams of adjacent rows of blocks, or rows within blocks, in opposite directions. The pressed seams will fit together snugly, producing precise intersections.

• Press, don't iron. Bring the iron down gently and firmly. This is especially important if you are using steam.

• To press appliqués, lay a towel on the ironing board, turn the piece right side down on the towel, and press very gently on the back side.

ASSEMBLING QUILT TOPS

Lay out all the blocks for your quilt top using the quilt diagram or photo as a guide to placement. Pin and sew the blocks together in vertical or horizontal rows for straight-set quilts and in diagonal rows for diagonal-set quilts. Press the seam allowances in opposite directions from row to row so that the seams will fit together snugly when rows are joined.

To keep a large quilt top manageable, join rows into pairs first and then join the pairs. When pressing a completed quilt top, press on the back side first, carefully clipping and removing hanging threads; then press the front.

MITERING BORDERS

Step 1: Start by measuring the length of your finished quilt top through the center. Add to that figure two times the width of the border, plus 5 inches extra. This is the length you need to cut the two side borders. For example, if the quilt top is 48 inches long and the border is 4 inches wide, you need two borders that are each 61 inches long (48 + 4 + 4 + 5 = 61). In the same manner, calculate the length of the top and bottom borders, then cut the borders.

Step 2: Sew each of the borders to the quilt top, beginning and ending the seams ¼ inch from the edge of the quilt. Press the border seams flat from the right side of the quilt.

Step 3: Working at one corner of the quilt, place one border on top of the adjacent border. Fold the top border under so that it meets the edge of the other border and forms a 45 degree angle, as shown in the diagram. If you are working with a plaid or striped border, check to make sure the stripes match along this folded edge. Press the fold in place.

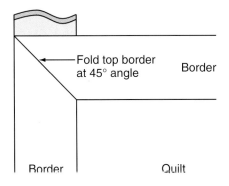

Step 4: Fold the quilt top with right sides together and align the edges of the borders. With the pressed fold as the corner seam line and the body of the quilt out of the way, sew from the inner corner to the outer corner, as shown in the diagram.

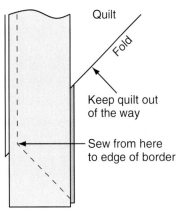

Step 5: Unfold the quilt and check to make sure that all points match and the miter is flat. Trim the border seam allowance to ¼ inch and press the seam open.

Step 6: Repeat Steps 3 through 5 for the three remaining borders.

MARKING QUILTING DESIGNS

To mark a quilting design, use a commercially made stencil, make your own stencil using a sheet of plastic, or trace the design from a book page. Use a nonpermanent marker, such as a silver or white pencil, chalk pencil, or chalk marker, that will be visible on the fabric. You can even mark with a 0.5 mm lead pencil, but be sure to mark lightly.

If you are using a quilt design from this book, either trace the design onto tracing paper or photocopy it. If the pattern will be used many times, glue it to cardboard to make it sturdy.

For light-color fabrics that you can see through, place the pattern under the quilt top and trace the quilting design directly onto the fabric. Mark in a thin, continuous line that will be covered by the quilting thread.

With dark fabrics, mark from the top by drawing around a hard-edged design template. To make a simple template, trace the design onto template plastic and cut it out around the outer edge. Trace around the template onto the fabric, then add inner lines by eye.

LAYERING AND BASTING

Carefully preparing the quilt top, batting, and backing will ensure that the finished quilt will lie flat and smooth. Place the backing wrong side up on a large table or clean floor. Center the batting on the backing and smooth out any wrinkles. Center the quilt top right side up on the batting; smooth it out and remove any loose threads.

If you plan to hand quilt, baste the quilt with thread. Use a long darning needle and white thread. Baste outward from the center of the quilt in a grid of horizontal and vertical rows approximately 4 inches apart.

If you plan to machine quilt, baste with safety pins. Thread basting does not hold the layers securely enough during machine quilting, plus the thread is more difficult to remove when quilting is completed. Use rustproof nickel-plated brass safety pins in size #0, pinning from the center of the quilt out approximately every 3 inches.

HAND QUILTING

For best results, use a hoop or a frame to hold the quilt layers taut and smooth during quilting. Work with one hand on top of the quilt and the other hand underneath, guiding the needle. Don't worry about the size of your stitches in the beginning; concentrate on making them even, and they will get smaller over time.

Getting started: Thread a needle with quilting thread and knot the end. Insert the needle through the quilt top and batting about 1 inch away from where you will begin stitching. Bring the needle to the surface in position to make the first stitch. Gently tug on the thread to pop the knot through the quilt top and bury it in the batting.

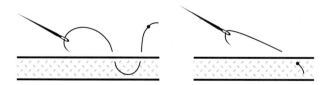

Taking the stitches: Insert the needle through the three layers of the quilt. When you feel the tip of the needle with your underneath finger, gently guide it back up through the quilt. When the needle comes through the top of the quilt, press your thimble on the end with the eye to guide it down again through the quilt layers. Continue to quilt in this manner, taking two or three small running stitches at a time.

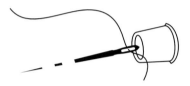

Ending a line of stitching: Bring the needle to the top of the quilt just past the last stitch. Make a knot at the surface by bringing the needle under the thread where it comes out of the fabric and up through the loop of thread it creates. Repeat this knot and insert the needle into the hole where the thread comes out of the fabric. Run the needle inside the batting for an inch and bring it back to the surface. Tug gently on the thread to pop the knot into the batting layer. Clip the thread.

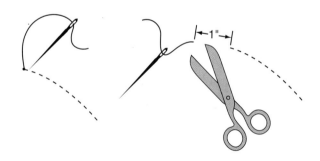

MACHINE QUILTING

For best results when doing machine-guided quilting, use a walking foot (also called an even feed foot) on your sewing machine. For free-motion quilting, use a darning or machine-embroidery foot.

Use thread to match the fabric colors, or use clear nylon thread in the top of the machine and a white or colored thread in the bobbin. To secure the thread at the beginning of a line of stitches, adjust the stitch length on your machine to make several very short stitches, then gradually increase to the regular stitch length. As you near the end of the line, gradually reduce the stitch length so that the last few stitches are very short.

For machine-guided quilting, keep the feed dogs up and move all three layers as smoothly as you can under the needle. To turn a corner in a quilting design, stop with the needle inserted in the fabric, raise the foot, pivot the quilt, lower the foot, and continue stitching.

For free-motion quilting, disengage the feed dogs so you can manipulate the quilt freely as you stitch. Guide the quilt under the needle with both hands, coordinating the speed of the needle with the movement of the quilt to create stitches of consistent length.

MAKING AND ATTACHING BINDING

Double-fold binding, which is also called French-fold binding, can be made from either straight-grain or bias strips. To make double-fold binding, cut strips of fabric four times the finished width of the binding, plus seam allowance. In general, cut strips 2 inches wide for quilts with thin batting and $2\frac{1}{4}$ inches wide for quilts with thicker batting.

Making Straight-Grain Binding

To make straight-grain binding, cut crosswise strips from the binding fabric in the desired width. Sew them together end to end with diagonal seams.

Place the strips with right sides together so that each strip is set in $\frac{1}{4}$ inch from the end of the other strip. Sew a diagonal seam and trim the excess fabric, leaving a $\frac{1}{4}$-inch seam allowance.

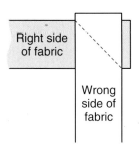

Right side of fabric

Wrong side of fabric

Making Continuous Bias Binding

Bias binding can be cut in one long strip from a square of fabric that has been cut apart and resewn into a tube. To estimate the number of inches of binding a particular square will produce, use this formula:

Multiply the length of one side by the length of another side, and divide the result by the width of binding you want. Using a 30-inch square and $2\frac{1}{4}$-inch binding as an example: $30 \times 30 = 900 \div 2\frac{1}{4} = 400$ inches of binding.

Step 1: To make bias binding, cut a square in half diagonally to get two triangles. Place the two triangles right sides together as shown and sew with a $\frac{1}{4}$-inch seam. Open out the two pieces and press the seam open.

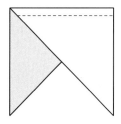

Step 2: Mark cutting lines on the wrong side of the fabric in the desired binding width. Mark the lines parallel to the bias edges.

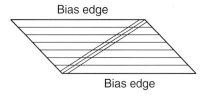

Bias edge

Bias edge

Step 3: Fold the fabric with right sides together, bringing the two nonbias edges together and offsetting them by one strip width (shown at the top of page 122). Pin the edges together, creating a tube, and sew with a $\frac{1}{4}$-inch seam. Press the seam open.

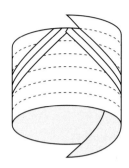

Step 4: Cut on the marked lines, turning the tube to cut one long bias strip.

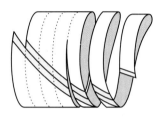

Attaching the Binding

Trim excess batting and backing even with the quilt top. For double-fold binding, fold the long binding strip in half lengthwise, wrong sides together, and press. Beginning in the middle of a side, not in a corner, place the strip right sides together with the quilt top, align the raw edges, and pin.

Step 1: Fold over approximately 1 inch at the beginning of the strip and begin stitching ½ inch from the fold. Sew the binding to the quilt, using a ¼-inch seam and stitching through all layers.

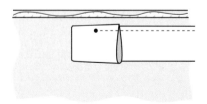

Step 2: As you approach a corner, stop stitching ¼ inch from the raw edge of the corner. Backstitch and remove the quilt from the machine. Fold the binding strip up at a 45 degree angle, as shown in the following diagram on the left. Fold the strip back down so there is a fold at the upper

edge, as shown on the right. Begin sewing at the top edge of the quilt, continuing to the next corner. Miter all four corners in this manner.

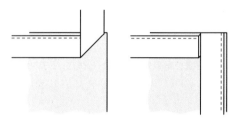

Step 3: To finish the binding seam, overlap the folded-back beginning section with the ending section. Stitch across the fold, allowing the end to extend approximately ½ inch beyond the beginning.

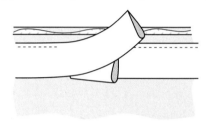

Step 4: Turn the binding to the back of the quilt and blindstitch the folded edge in place, covering the machine stitches with the folded edge. Fold in the adjacent sides on the back and take several stitches in the miter. In the same way, add several stitches to the miters on the front.

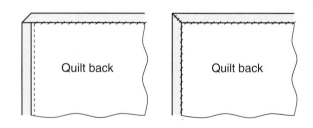

SIGNING YOUR QUILT

Be sure to sign and date your finished quilt. Your finishing touch can be a simple signature in permanent ink or an elaborate inked or embroidered label. Add any other pertinent details that can help family members or quilt collectors 100 years from now understand what went into your labor of love.